AEROBICS
THEORY & PRACTICE
SELF-STUDY WORKBOOK

Aerobics and Fitness Association of America

Edited by Peg Angsten, R.N. and Mary Beth Ferrari

10 9 8 7 6 5 4

PRINTED IN THE UNITED STATES OF AMERICA

ISBN 0-937359-19-X

DIRECTIONS TO THE STUDENT

T his Workbook consists of 27 self-instructional units which have been designed to guide you through the acquisition of knowledge and skills related to the instruction of an aerobic exercise class. You are encouraged to proceed at your own rate and to answer all of the questions in a unit before checking your responses in the answer key.

It is the intention of this Workbook to clearly delineate those chapters of the textbook **Aerobics: Theory & Practice** that provide the essential core of AFAA's National Primary Certification written exam. Questions and answers selected enable the student to identify and assimilate cogent material presented in the textbook.

The clinical assignments in each unit relate to many of the fundamentals taught during the practical demonstrations in AFAA's Instructor Training Program and during the Certification Workshop. However, it is not the goal of this Workbook to prepare the student for the practical component of the Certification procedure. Most units contain the following:

1. An overall cognitive objective to identify the focus of the chapter
2. Ten multiple choice questions
3. Eight true and false items
4. Five fill-in questions
5. Two clinical discussions/assignments
6. Answers to all questions, with references to page(s) in **Aerobics: Theory & Practice** where explanations are found.

After reading a chapter in the textbook, complete the matching self-study unit, and work with the material until you are confident about your answers. It is suggested that you write each of your answers on a separate piece of paper before you check the answers located at the end of each chapter. Difficulty with the unit indicates a need to re-examine the material in the textbook.

You now have the most complete tools available to exercise instructors, and you are now ready to begin.

Peg Angsten, R.N.
Mary Beth Ferrari

PREFACE

Aerobics: Theory & Practice and this accompanying Self-Study Workbook provide a unique approach to the study and practice of aerobic exercise instruction. With the publishing of this self-instructional guide, AFAA has offered the first comprehensive educational package for the instructor. From textbook, to study guide, to a newly revised set of Standards and Guidelines—the instructor finally has resources and tools that will guide him or her through the theoretical and practical training that is necessary to stay at the head of the class. The consistency reflected in all these educational materials provides an unprecedented continuity for AFAA's National Certification exam procedure.

It is indeed an honor to display the prestigious seal of the National Fitness Foundation on the textbook and this Workbook. The seal represents recognition by the NFF of the value of the information in this book.

I wish to thank Peg Angsten, R.N. and Mary Beth Ferrari for their diligent editing skills in transforming the essential chapters of the textbook into this step-by-step guide. I also wish to acknowledge AFAA's team of advisors and reviewers: Neil Sol, Ph.D., John Black, M.S., R.P.T., William Beam, Ph.D., Marti West and Linda Shelton for their careful critique and helpful comments. Marti and Linda are also highly commended for organizing the collection of research and industry experience that went into the updated edition of AFAA's Basic Exercise Standards and Guidelines. This entire body of knowledge once again reflects the vast experience and knowledge of the original 17 authors compiled in **Aerobics: Theory & Practice.**

I would also like to express appreciation to AFAA's students—a collection of hard working, dedicated individuals who comprise AFAA itself. It has always been the goal of AFAA to recognize and reward the achievements of these relatively new professionals. Serving this profession through the development of national standards and educational materials, the Aerobics and Fitness Association of America is the sum of the efforts of thousands of committed professionals. Finally, I would like to thank Angel Martinez, Vice President of Reebok International and the entire Educational Division of Reebok for their generous sponsorship of this Workbook, and for their continued support of AFAA's educational programs.

Linda D. Pfeffer, R.N., President
Sherman Oaks, California

Part A

Essentials of Aerobic Exercise

Chapter 1

What is Aerobic Exercise?

Today, aerobic exercise is being embraced by many Americans who want to improve their everyday lives. Although aerobics is widely used, it is frequently not well understood.

I. Multiple Choice Questions

Read each question carefully and choose the best response. Circle your answer.

1. Currently, Americans are experiencing a nationwide interest in aerobic conditioning. Aerobic activities possess the following characteristics in common:
   a. a continous, submaximal level of energy expenditures.
   b. the use of large muscle groups.
   c. occurrence with oxygen or in the presence of oxygen.
   d. all of the above.

2. Aerobic energy production requires a constant and adequate supply of oxygen. To meet this demand, the following body systems must be utilized (Choose two):
   a. respiratory
   b. digestive
   c. cardiovascular
   d. nervous

3. During the functioning of the body's oxygen delivery system, all of the following activities take place EXCEPT:
   a. oxygen is attached to hemoglobin molecules and is carried throughout the blood stream.

b. stored glucose is broken down into carbon dioxide, lactic acid, and water.

c. oxygen is taken from the outside environment into the circulatory system.

d. through a process called diffusion, carbon dioxide is removed from the blood.

4. All of the following statements help to define the term cardiac output EXCEPT:

a. determined by multiplying the heart rate by the amount of blood pumped out of the heart per beat.

b. relates to the functional capacity of the circulatory system to meet the demands of aerobic endurance activity.

c. blood surges out of the left ventricle into the aorta, distending it and creating pressure.

d. the amount of blood the heart pumps per minute.

5. Energy comes into the body in the form of:

a. carbohydrates   b. proteins

c. fats   d. all of the above

6. Choose the body part that is not a storage site for energy.

a. muscle   b. nerves

c. blood   d. liver

7. The body manufactures a chemical compound known as adenosine triphosphate or ATP. Which of the following statements does not characterize ATP?

a. ATP is stored in all cells and is used for all the energy-requiring processes within the cell.

b. the amount of available ATP for immediate use that is stored in our body at any one time is about sixteen ounces.

c. the breakdown of ATP enables a muscle to shorten or contract.

d. ATP is constantly being resynthesized in the cells, providing a continous supply of energy.

8. Glycolysis is a series of reactions that cause:

a. the breakdown of a glucose molecule.

b. the production of ATP and lactic acid.

c. rapid, but limited amounts of energy for muscular activity.

d. all of the above.

9. The ability to utilize stored body fat as a primary source of energy is one of the more important characteristics of:

a. the anaerobic energy system.

        b. cellular respiration or metabolism.

        c. the lactic acid system.

        d. the aerobic energy pathway.

   10. Continuous aerobic conditioning will produce increases in the following:

        a. maximal oxygen uptake.

        b. total blood volume and amount of hemoglobin.

        c. maximum cardiac output.

        d. all of the above.

II. True or False Items

Read each statement carefully. If correct, write TRUE on the line provided; if incorrect, write FALSE on the line provided.

1. ___T___ Participation in aerobic activity requires a conditioned cardiovascular system capable of supplying adequate amounts of oxygen to the working muscles.

2. ___T___ The system by which the lungs bring oxygen into the circulatory system is called pulmonary ventilation.

3. ___T___ At rest, the cardiac output of trained individuals is different from that of sedentary individuals.

4. ___T___ The liberation of chemical energy from glucose is called cellular respiration or metabolism.

5. ___T___ When ATP in a muscle cell is broken down, the energy released activates the contractile elements in the muscle fibers.

6. ___F___ During prolonged exercise, most of the energy requirement is generated by the anaerobic energy system.

7. ___F___ During submaximal aerobic activity, the trained person will use less fatty acids for fuel than the untrained person.

8. ___F___ Studies indicate that running is definitely the best form of aerobic conditioning.

III. Fill-In Questions

Read each statement carefully and fill in the space provided with the best response.

1. Define the term "aerobic activity." _____

_____

2. List at least five different modes of exercise that can be con-

sidered aerobic activities. _____

_____

3. Discuss the relationship between cardiac output and the functional capacity of the circulatory system to meet the demands of aerobic endurance activity._____

_____

4. What is the primary purpose of metabolism? _____

_____

5. Discuss duration of training with regard to aerobic activity and the nonathletic adult. _____

_____

IV. Clinical Discussions/Assignments

1. Discuss the various factors that affect aerobic training. - p.8
2. Design and develop a daily exercise routine for a senior citizen whose aerobic fitness has declined.

CHAPTER ONE ANSWERS

I.   Multiple Choice Questions

1. d - p.3
2. a,c - p.4
3. b - p.4
4. c - p.4
5. d - p.5
6. b - p.5
7. b - p.6
8. d - p.6
9. d - p.7
10. d - p.7

II.   True or False Items

1. True - p.3
2. True - p.4
3. False- p.5
4. True - p.5
5. True - p.6
6. False- p.7
7. False- p.8
8. False- p.9

III.   Fill-In Questions

1. Any activity that uses large muscle groups, can be maintained continuously, is rhythmic and utilizes the aerobic energy production system. - p.8
2. Running, walking, bicycling, swimming and rowing - p.3 & 9
3. As exercise intensity increases, the demand for oxygenated bloodflow to the exercising muscle increases. Increases in cardiac output are met by both an increase in heart rate and in stroke volume. - p.5
4. To supply the energy needed to carry out the mechanical work of muscular contraction. - p.5
5. 20-60 minutes of continuous aerobic activity. Low-to-moderate intensity activity of longer duration is recommended for the nonathletic adult. - p.8

Chapter 2

Anatomy and Physiology of Aerobic Exercise

At the completion of this chapter, you should be able to demonstrate a knowledge of anatomical and physiological principles of aerobic exercise.

I. Multiple Choice Questions

Read each question carefully and choose the best response. Circle your answer.

1. Bone density is directly related to:
   a. calcium content
   b. weight bearing exercise
   c. aging
   d. all of the above
2. The skeletal system can be weakened by:
   a. inadequate rest
   b. too much exercise
   c. poor nutrition
   d. all of the above
3. Aerobic instructors should limit classes per day to:
   a. no more than 4
   b. 5 or less
   c. daily count is not as important as weekly total
   d. no more than 3
4. Exercise stress can be modified by which of the following?
   a. footwear and floor surfaces
   b. duration and intensity
   c. proper biomechanics
   d. all of the above
5. Exercise fatigue is experienced when a build up of the following end product is excessive:
   a. pyruvic acid
   b. hydrogen ions
   c. lactic acid
   d. ADP

6. Straight leg sit-ups should be avoided so that:
   a. the knee ligaments are not strained
   b. the iliopsoas becomes the primary mover
   c. the rectus abdominis is primary mover
   d. iliopsoas and r. abdominis work together
7. Ballistic exercise implies:
   a. muscle isolation
   b. concentric contraction
   c. initiation of the stretch reflex
   d. eccentric contraction
8. The fastest way for the cells to provide energy to resynthesize ATP is by using the stored energy in this chemical:
   a. ADP   b. oxygen
   c. creatine phosphate   d. chemical food bonds
9. Glycolysis is the breaking apart of which substance:
   a. glucose   b. free radicals
   c. complex carbohydrate   d. amino acid
10. Strengthening of which muscle helps prevent dislocation of the patella:
   a. vastus lateralis   b. vastus medialis
   c. hamstring   d. gastrocnemius

II. True or False Items

Read each statement carefully. If correct, write TRUE on the line provided; if incorrect, write FALSE on the line provided.

1. __T__ Support is the single most important factor in aerobic shoe design.
2. __F__ The axial skeleton is comprised of bones surrounding the axis of the body, which is the imaginary line running horizontally along the body's center of gravity.
3. __T__ The appendicular skeleton contains the bones of the arms and shoulders, legs and pelvis.
4. __T__ Foramina are openings in the vertebrae through which the spinal cord passes.
5. __F__ Although it is not always recommended, proper pelvic alignment can only be achieved with the knees hyperextended.

6. __F__ The knee joint connects the femur to the fibula.
7. __T__ Sway back could be the result of a very tight erector spinae.
8. __F__ The efferent nerves carry information about your body's position in space.

III.   Fill-In Questions

Read each statement carefully and fill in the space provided with the best response.

1. Primary support for the vertebrae is provided by which ligament? _____

   _____

2. Define energy. _____

   _____

3. Name the three major pathways that may be utilized to replenish ATP. _____

   _____

4. Describe the best means for maximizing fat utilization. ____

   _____

5. Explain the risks involved with head circling, the plough and standing toe touches. _____

   _____

IV.   Clinical Discussions/Assignments

1. Discuss the importance of supporting the body's weight when exercising in an upright posture.
2. Explain how intensity influences energy metabolism in regard to aerobic versus anaerobic exercise.

CHAPTER TWO ANSWERS

I. Multiple Choice Questions

1. d - p.12
2. d - p.12
3. d - p.13
4. d - p.14
5. c - p.33
6. c - p.37
7. c - p.37
8. c - p.30
9. a - p.31
10. b - p.28

II. True or False Items

1. True - p.14
2. False - p.15
3. True - p.15
4. True - p.16
5. False - p.28
6. False - p.25
7. True - p.23
8. False - p.21

III. Fill-In Questions

1. Posterior longitudinal ligament which tapers down to its smallest size in the lumbar spine. - p.19
2. The ability or capacity to do work, which is force through a distance. - p.29
3. 1) ATP-CP system, 2) Lactic acid system, and 3) Aerobic metabolism. - p.30-32
4. Long duration exercise programs with submaximal intensity, performed for at least 30 continuous minutes about 4 times per week. - p.33
5. 1) Excessive strain on the 7th cervical vertebra; 2) pinching of the vertebral artery; 3) compressive forces in the intervertebral discs of the lumbar spine. - p.17-19

Chapter 3

Medical Considerations of Aerobic Exercise

U pon completion of this unit, you should understand the basic physiology of exercise and its benefits for the cardiovascular system.

I.   Multiple Choice Questions

Read each question carefully and choose the best response. Circle your answer.

1. A progressive decline in maximal oxygen uptake occurs with aging. This process can be modified through:
   a. maximal exercise   b. regular submaximal exercise
   c. deep breathing exercises   d. frequent stress testing
2. Inevitable side effects of any training program include:
   a. excessive anaerobic metabolism   b. progressive fatigue
   c. lactate accumulation   d. none of the above
3. Exercise-induced anaphylaxis is a condition which should alert the instructor to:
   a. emergency medical treatment
   b. harmless blotchy patches on the skin
   c. low doses of antihistamine   d. CPR
4. Whenever a pulse rate fails to return to below 60% of the maximal predicted heart rate at least five minutes after exercise, the exerciser should:
   a. lower the intensity
   b. lengthen static stretching period
   c. return to peak exercise
   d. seek medical clearance

5. Urticaria, like many exercise-induced ailments, can be treated successfully. The first signs of urticaria are:
   a. histamine release with sneezing, watery eyes.
   b. blotchy red rash and itching.
   c. tightness in the throat and difficulty breathing.
   d. tightness and squeezing in the chest.

6. Which of the following is not considered a major risk factor for cardiovascular disease:
   a. hypertension
   b. increased cholesterol levels
   c. frequent alcohol intake
   d. smoking

7. Pulse rates in individuals who overtrain may show the following pattern:
   a. progressively falling when measured first thing in the morning.
   b. slightly rapid, indicating insufficient recovery.
   c. no pattern can be detected.
   d. slower than usual in the morning.

8. Which of the following is the predicted value for 60% of the maximum heart rate for a 45-year-old untrained individual?
   a. 118
   b. 109
   c. 105
   d. 111

9. What are the three essential elements in gas exchange between the cell mitochrondria and external environment?
   a. muscle, contraction, and circulation.
   b. muscle, circulation, and inspiration.
   c. muscle, circulation, and ventilation.
   d. muscle, contraction, and digestion.

10. There is some evidence which suggests that warm-up and cooldown may be safety factors against which of the following:
    a. hives
    b. asthma
    c. analphylaxis
    d. arrhythmias

II. True or False Items

Read each statement carefully. If correct, write TRUE on the line provided; if incorrect, write FALSE on the line provided.

1. ____T____ A greater amount of oxygen is extracted from the blood per heartbeat as a result of aerobic training.
2. ____F____ Resting heart rate should be determined about one hour after awakening.
3. ____F____ An oxygen uptake of 20 ml O_2/kg/min would be considered an average range for a 40-year-old.
4. ____T____ An optimal training heart rate range for the healthy young adult is 60-85% of the maximal predicted heart rate.
5. ____T____ Individuals with exercise-induced asthma often have a background of allergies.
6. ____T____ The most common cause of sudden death in individuals over 40 is coronary artery disease.
7. ____F____ Thickening of the heart muscle wall is called hypotrophic cardiomyopathy.
8. ____F____ Cigarette smoking is considered a minor risk for development of coronary heart disease.

III. Fill-In Questions

Read each statement carefully and fill in the space provided with the best response.

1. What are four danger signs which may indicate cardio-vascular disease? _____

_____

2. Sweat is composed primarily of what element? _____

_____

3. What is the basic rule of thumb for adequate hydration before exercise? _____

_____

4. Briefly describe the process of re-oxygenating the blood.

_____

_____

5. What is the recommended resting pulse following a session of vigorous exercise? _____

_____

CHAPTER THREE ANSWERS

I.   Multiple Choice Questions

1. b - p.44
2. d - p.45
3. a - p.49
4. a - p.45
5. b - p.49
6. c - p.47
7. b - p.45
8. c - p.45
9. c - p.43
10. d - p.48

II.   True or False Items

1. True - p.44
2. False - p.45
3. False - p.43
4. True - p.44
5. True - p.48
6. True - p.47
7. False - p.47
8. False - p.47

III.   Fill-In Questions

1. Irregular heart rate, palpitations, chest discomfort and sudden breathlessness. - p.47
2. Water - p.46
3. Drink 8 to 10 ounces of water 10 to 20 minutes before beginning a workout. - p.46
4. Deoxygenated blood is returned to the heart for circulation to the lungs where carbon dioxide is exchanged with oxygen. Oxygen-rich blood is then returned to the heart and pumped throughout the body. - p.41
5. The resting pulse should return to 60% of the peak exercise heart rate within 3 to 5 minutes after completion of a workout. - p.45

Chapter 4

Applied Physiological Principles
of Aerobic Exercise

U pon completion of this unit, you should understand the physiological process of aerobic training, steady state and anaerobic threshold. You should also be aware of the positive outcomes and possible complications associated with aerobic exercise.

I.   Multiple Choice Questions

Read each question carefully and choose the best response. Circle your answer.

1. The final heart rate as the class members are preparing to leave should be at or about what level:
   a. just below the target range of 70 to 80 percent.
   b. below 60% of maximal heart rate.
   c. equal to the resting heart rate taken first thing in the morning.
   d. overall fatigue is the best gauge for recovery assessment.
2. Whenever blood is pooled in the extremities, the following condition(s) may arise:
   a. fainting
   b. arrythmias or irregular heart rhythms
   c. inadequate amounts of blood to the brain
   d. all of the above
3. Breath-holding and straining to execute a maneuver can cause which of the following:
   a. elevation or irregular heart rate
   b. faster accumulation of an acidotic blood PH

c. excessive stress placed on the heart

d. all of the above

4. Which of the following best describes anaphylactic reactions?

a. severe allergic reactions that may result in death if untreated

b. outpouching of gas in the colon

c. hypoglycemic reaction causing lightheadedness and shaking

d. fainting and loss of consciousness from insufficient cooldown.

5. The average healthy young adult can usually tolerate a training heart rate of 70 to 85% of maximal heart rate. For beginners, this number can be adjusted to:

a. 75 to 85% of maximal heart rate

b. maximal heart rate is what beginners usually achieve

c. use perceived exertion only for beginners

d. 60 to 70% as a good starting range for beginners

6. Monitoring the heart rate in class is done by monitoring the pulse. AFAA recommends which of the following methods of pulse taking:

a. Count the pulse for 6 seconds and multiply by 10

b. Count the pulse for 15 seconds and multiply by 4

c. Count the pulse for 10 seconds and multiply by 6

d. Any of the above is approved for exercise classes

7. Anaerobic workouts differ from aerobic workouts in which of the following ways:

a. aerobic workouts tend to raise blood pressure more significantly

b. both heart rate and blood pressure are higher in aerobic work compared to anaerobic work

c. persons with high blood pressure are cautioned against aerobic work

d. both heart rate and blood pressure are higher in anaerobic work compared to aerobic work

8. The simplest, initial screening for beginning participants would be which of the following:

a. completion of a health information form

b. personal interview

c. reading the results of an exercise stress test

d. signed waiver and release form

9. Although it is ideal for both instructors and students to accept responsibility for a safe workout, ultimate responsibility for educating class participants rests with:
   a. the participant himself
   b. the club owner or manager
   c. the instructor
   d. the participant's regular physician
10. Signs of exercise intolerance include which of the following:
   a. severe fatigue and labored breathing
   b. pain and staggering
   c. both a and b
   d. neither a nor b

II. True or False Items

Read each statement carefully. If correct, write TRUE on the line provided; if incorrect, write FALSE on the line provided.

1. __F__ Studies have finally eliminated the link between definite risk of cardiovascular complications and exercise.
2. __T__ Regardless of age, individuals should be screened by a physician prior to beginning an exercise program, if they have a pre-existing medical condition.
3. __F__ Saunas should be avoided following vigorous exercise due to excessive vasoconstriction.
4. __F__ If the heart rate exceeds 60% of maximum five minutes after aerobic work, it more than likely reflects the need for a higher target heart rate.
5. __T__ Cardiac-related pain can be present in the left shoulder and the jaw.
6. __F__ Placements of fingers on both sides of the neck insures the best detection for carotid pulse.
7. __F__ AFAA recommends the neck as the primary site for pulse taking.
8. __F__ RICE stands for Rest, Ice, Compression and Exercise.

III. Fill-In Questions

Read each statement carefully and fill in the space provided with the best response.

1. Explain the purpose for the pre-exercise medical examination.

_____

_____

_____

2. Give three benefits of a proper warm-up period.

_____

_____

3. A student complains that after one year she is not gaining any of the benefits of exercise that you described. She attends class once a week. What might you discuss with her? _____

_____

_____

4. One student has not taken classes for approximately 12 weeks due to a sprained ankle. He can expect what kind of loss of cardiovascular benefits due to detraining?

_____

_____

5. Define a "side-stitch" and give one possible cause.

_____

_____

V.   Clinical Discussions/Assignments

1. A diabetic asks you when he should eat his meals and take his medication in relation to taking an aerobic exercise class. Discuss the best response.
2. Explain the rationale, physiology and best method of monitoring a proper cooldown period.

ANSWERS FOR CHAPTER FOUR

I. Multiple Choice Questions

1. b - p.57
2. d - p.57
3. d - p.56
4. a - p.62
5. d - p.59
6. c - p.58
7. d - p.56
8. a - p.52
9. c - p.63
10. c - p.60

II. True or False Items

1. False - p.52
2. True - p.52
3. False - p.57
4. False - p.57
5. True - p.66
6. False - p.65
7. False - p.65
8. False - p.63

III. Fill-In Questions

1. The examination assists the participant in identifying any pre-existing conditions, such as anemia, heart disease and arthritis, that might hamper a positive outcome to the program. - p.52
2. 1) increased blood blow to the working muscles; 2) increased core temperature producing increased muscular efficiency; and 3) decreased potential for injuries due to their increased elasticity. - p. 55
3. A regular attendance of three to five one-hour sessions a week is necessary to realize the benefits of aerobic classes. - p.54
4. Four to 12 weeks of detraining has been shown to result in a 50% reduction in cardiorespiratory fitness. - p.54
5. Sudden sharp pains in the upper part of the abdomen during the initial stages of exercise. One likely cause is cramping of the diaphragm. - p.62

Chapter 5

Body Composition

U pon completion of this unit, you should understand the concepts of overweight versus overfat, methods of analyzing body composition and desirable ranges of body fat for men and women.

I. Multiple Choice Questions

Read each question carefully and choose the best response. Circle your answer.

1. Body composition refers to the types and amount of tissues that make up the body. The four major tissue types are:
    a. muscle mass, bone mass, circulatory mass, and organ mass
    b. muscle mass, nerve mass, circulatory mass, and organ mass
    c. muscle mass, bone mass, fat mass, and organ mass
    d. muscle mass, bone mass, fat mass, and water mass
2. Normal menstrual cycles appear to be related to which of the following:
    a. critical fat threshold of less than 17%
    b. a complex interaction between physical, hormonal, nutritional, and other factors
    c. both a and b
    d. menstrual cycles are not affected by exercise, as evidenced by women athletes with normal cycles
3. When performing skinfold measurements, it is important to remember:
    a. a minimum of two measurements should be taken at each site

  b. placement of calipers is not as important as the number of times a site is measured

  c. do not release the caliper grip fully or full tension will be lost

  d. take an average of at least two measurements regardless of the range

4. Suprailium skinfold site on women requires which type of pinch:

  a. horizontal above waist line

  b. vertical below waist line

  c. diagonal near the waist line

  d. vertical at hip level

5. The term overweight refers to:

  a. the composition of body weight into lean weight and fat weight

  b. the amount of muscle mass, bone mass, and body organ mass

  c. weight based on a standard of sex, height, and frame

  d. the amount of body fat that may be stored on the body

6. The lowest lean weight in healthy women is which of the following ranges:

  a. 5% - 8% essential fat content

  b. 8% - 10% essential fat content

  c. 10% - 12% essential fat content

  d. anything above 2%

7. The most accurate method of assessing body composition is:

  a. hydrostatic weighing

  b. skinfold measurement

  c. height and weight tables

  d. abdominal girth measurements

8. Skinfold measurements can be affected by which of the following:

  a. inaccurate calculations

  b. technique of practitioner

  c. selection of proper site

  d. all of the above

9. The fat commonly known as essential fat is stored in which of the following places:

  a. bone marrow, heart, liver and lungs

  b. subcutaneous tissues

  c. hips, thighs and buttocks in females

  d. abdomen in men

10. Storage fat, versus essential fat, serves the following function in the body:
   a. is used for short-term activity, such as sprinting
   b. carries on normal functions for the internal organs
   c. serves as shock absorber to cushion and protect bones, muscles, and internal organs from injury
   d. has no bearing on heat transfer

II. True or False Items

Read each statement carefully. If correct, write TRUE on the line provided; if incorrect, write FALSE.

1. ____F____ A body fat percent of 14 is considered very good for a 19-year-old male.

2. ____T____ The primary reason adults gain more fat as they age is that there is a tendency towards less activity as one ages.

3. ____F____ The formula for calculating desirable body weight is: desirable weight equals lean body weight divided by 1 minus the percent of present body fat.

4. ____T____ Optimal body fat levels should be determined for each individual rather than implied from tables.

5. ____F____ A skinfold is the naturally occurring flap of tissue at varying sites on each individual.

6. ____F____ The distribution for fat storage differs between men and women, but remains the same for women of any age.

7. ____F____ The best way for an obese person to lose weight is to begin a 5-day per week running regimen.

8. ____T____ Lean body weight component consists of 40%-50% muscle mass.

III. Fill-In Questions

Read each statement carefully and fill in the space provided with the best response.

1. Describe the best way to lose excessive body fat. _____

_____

2. What is the association between low body fat levels and amenorrhea? _____

_____

3. What is the prevalence of obesity in developed countries?

_____

_____

4. List the three anatomical sites for determining body fat on men with a skinfold caliper. _____

_____

_____

5. Explain why excessive body fat may create heat injury while exercising. _____

_____

IV.   Clinical Discussions/Assignment

1. Describe the difference between overweight and overfat. Discuss the problems of reliance upon height and weight tables.
2. Determine someone's percent body fat and lean body weight by using skin caliper measurements.

ANSWERS FOR CHAPTER FIVE

I. Multiple Choice Questions

1. c - p.69
2. b - p.71
3. a - p.73
4. c - p.75
5. c - p.68
6. c - p.71
7. a - p.69
8. d - p.72
9. a - p.70
10. c - p.70

II. True or False Items

1. False - p.77
2. True - p.77
3. False - p.78
4. True - p.79
5. False - p.72
6. False - p.70
7. False - p.79
8. True - p.69

III. Fill-In Questions

1. Combination of diet and exercise is the most effective way to lose body fat safely. A weight loss in excess of 2 pounds per week is probably not a fat loss. - p.79
2. A body fat below 17% fat can trigger hormonal and metabolic disturbances that affect the normal menstrual cycle, according to one study. - p.79
3. It is estimated that approximately 35% of the adult populations in developed countries are obese. - p.78
4. 1) chest, between the axillary line and the nipple; 2) abdomen, 1" from the umbilicus; and 3) thigh, vertical fold on the midthigh. - p.76
5. Heat which must be transferred from working muscles to the periphery (skin) is impeded by large amounts of fat in the subcutaneous tissues. Excess body fat also adds to the metabolic cost of the activity, creating more heat as a by-product of exercise. - p.70

Chapter 6

General Nutritional Needs

U pon completion of this unit, you should understand proper nutrition as a source of energy for exercise, as well as normal daily needs.

I. Multiple-Choice Questions

Read each question carefully and choose the best response. Circle your answer.

1. Which of the following plays a vital role in the human diet, but is not absorbed and therefore cannot be considered a nutrient by definition?
   a. protein b. carbohydrates
   c. vitamins d. fiber
2. Water is the most basic of nutrient needs. It is essential to life because it:
   a. contributes to the structure and form of the body.
   b. provides the liquid environment for all processes.
   c. aids in regulation of body temperature.
   d. all of the above.
3. For each 1,000 calories consumed, one needs the following amount of water intake primarily from foods and water-producing foods.
   a. one cup b. one-half gallon
   c. one quart d. none of the above
4. This nutrient makes up the basic structure of all living cells and is essential for formation and maintenance of the organism.
   a. minerals b. carbohydrates
   c. protein d. fats
5. Current health standards recommend that approximately 55%-60% of our daily caloric intake be consumed as:
   a. protein b. fats

c. minerals   d. carbohydrates

6. Fiber has a distinctive role as it is transported through the gastrointestinal tract. In general, fiber functions as:
   a. a bulk agent, easing elimination and decreasing appetite.
   b. an agent that decreases the rate of absorption of glucose from meals.
   c. a chelating agent, decreasing the absorption of cholesterol and an excess of vital minerals from the diet
   d. all of the above.

7. Fats combine with other nutrients to form important structural compounds. Which of the following is not among this group:
   a. amino acids   b. steroids
   c. bile   d. vitamin D

8. The following is not characteristic of vitamins:
   a. cannot be manufactured by the human body
   b. are better absorbed when obtained through natural food
   c. aid in regulating body temperature
   d. classified as water or fat soluble

9. Minerals are not:
   a. organic compounds
   b. control agents in body reactions
   c. present in two main groups: major and trace
   d. cooperative factors in energy production and body building

10. In light of current research, the current recommended daily allowance for calcium will soon be:
    a. lowered   b. raised
    c. eliminated altogether   d. none of the above

II. True or False Items

Read each statement carefully. If correct, write TRUE on the line provided; if incorrect, write FALSE on the line provided.

1. ___T___ Water is the most abundant body constituent.

2. ___F___ Proteins of animal origin (meat, poultry, fish, milk, cheese and egg) are deficient in one or more essential amino acids and are therefore considered incomplete proteins.

3. ___T___ Physical trauma dramatically increases our protein requirements since protein is needed for repair.

4. ___T___ The power for body work can simply and rapidly be derived from carbohydrate foods.

5. __F__ The average American's diet contains approximately 10-20 grams of fiber per day which is more than sufficient to meet the body's need for dietary fiber.

6. __F__ All fats are soluble in water.

7. __T__ Vitamins require no digestive process and are absorbed intact into the bloodstream.

8. __T__ The more restrictive the diet, the more difficult it becomes to reach balanced nutrition.

III.   Fill-In Questions

Read each statement carefully and fill in the space provided with the best response.

1. List the seven nutrients necessary for life. _____

_____

_____

2. The quality standard for a complete protein containing the best ratio and quantity of essential amino acids is the

_____

_____

3. The "Daily Food Guide" organizes foods which make similar nutritional contributions into which four large groups?

_____

_____

4. Discuss the importance of carbohydrates in the diet.

_____

_____

5. What food combinations will create the proper balance of essential amino acids for body needs in a vegetarian diet that eliminates all animal proteins? _____

_____

_____

IV.   Clinical Discussions/Assignments

1. Conduct the necessary research and plan one week's menu (breakfast, lunch, and dinner) for a teenager who is a lacto-ovo-vegetarian.

2. Complete the above assignment for an adult who is a strict vegetarian.

ANSWERS FOR CHAPTER SIX

I. Multiple-Choice Questions

1. d - p.81
2. d - p.82
3. c - p.82
4. c - p.82
5. d - p.85
6. d - p.86
7. a - p.86
8. c - p.87
9. a - p.89
10. b - p.92

II. True or False Items

1. True - p.82
2. False - p.83
3. True - p.83
4. True - p.85
5. False - p.86
6. False - p.86
7. True - p.87
8. True - p.93

III. Fill-In Questions

1. Protein, carbohydrates, fats, vitamins, minerals, fiber, and water. - p.81
2. egg albumin (egg white) - p.83
3. Fruits and vegetables, meat and other proteins, grains, and milk. - p.90
4. Energy for muscles and organs can be met by carbohydrates even in the absence of sufficient oxygen. Carbohydrates are important in the diet to avoid the unnecessary use of protein as an energy source. - p.85
5. Grains and legumes, nut seeds and vegetables - p.84

Chapter 7

Developing Endurance

Upon completion of this unit, you should understand the training effects of cardiovascular exercise. You should also understand the principles of overload and specificity, along with the guidelines for their application.

I. Multiple Choice Questions

Read each question carefully and choose the best response. Circle your answer.

1. A 28-year-old student tells you that she exercises one to two times a week, for 20 to 30 minutes and sustains heavy breathing and perspiration. Her resting heart rate is 80. Rate her fitness category, then determine the correct Karvonen-calculated target heart rate zone.
   a. 156-160   b. 160-164
   c. 147-158   d. 168-184

2. The best definition of overload principle can be summed up in which of the following descriptions:
   a. Specific types of training are dependent on specific use of working neuromuscular and skeletal systems.
   b. Varying the types of demands placed on the body will avoid prolonged plateaus.
   c. Positive adaptations may be lost if exercise is not performed on a regular basis.
   d. Adaptations occur as a result of increasing demands on a particular function.

3. Individuals in an excellent cardiovascular fitness category need to follow which of these recommendations:
   a. apply more overload to realize further improvement.
   b. reduce the amount of overload to avoid injury.
   c. vary the workout to train other sets of muscle groups.
   d. any of the above might be appropriate.

4. For individuals in a poor fitness category, frequency and duration guidelines should be the following:
   a. every other day, 10 minutes at THR.
   b. 2 days a week, one hour at THR.
   c. 5 days a week, 20 minutes at THR.
   d. 5 or 6 days a week, 10 minutes at THR.

5. For students who are unable to detect their pulse rates, the following method is acceptable for measuring exercise intensity:
   a. holding their breath, and determining the level of breathlessness for one minute.
   b. rating their fatigue on a 6-20 chart of perceived exertion scale.
   c. having medical personnel listen with a stethoscope to their heart at least once a week.
   d. try to obtain blood pressure instead of heart rate.

6. A less complicated type of heart rate formula than the Karvonen formula is which of the following:
   a. 220 – age = X. (70%-80%) X = THR.
   b. 220 – age = X. RHR plus (70%-80%) X = THR.
   c. 220 – age = X. X plus RHR (70%-80%) = THR.
   d. 220 – age = X. MHR – RHR (70%-80%) = THR.

7. Which of the following requires the body to make new adaptations?
   a. exercising at higher altitude.
   b. switching from running to race walking.
   c. alternating days off from exercise.
   d. all of the above.

8. Some individuals can exercise above their target heart rate due to:
   a. age-predicted maximum heart rates are simply an approximation that may not apply to each individual.
   b. some individuals have very high resting heart rates.
   c. both a and b are correct.
   d. only a is correct.

9. During vigorous exercise in the heat, blood is redirected according to which of the following:
   a. from the skin and peripheral tissues to the internal digestive organs and kidneys.
   b. from the organs and kidneys to the skin for heat dissipation.

    c. from the internal organs to the brain due to a greater
need for homeostatic control.

    d. the majority remains with the internal organs to avoid
heat exposure.

10. The amount of carbohydrates that can be stored within the
body is limited to approximately:

    a. a 30-minute supply.

    b. a two-hour supply.

    c. an unlimited supply.

    d. a six-hour supply.

II. True or False Items

Read each statement carefully. If correct, write TRUE on the
line provided; if incorrect, write FALSE.

1. _____ Perceived exertion ratings are the most accurate
means of measuring exercise intensity.

2. _____ Numerous studies have indicated that exercise for
40 minutes a day, 5 days a week is the minimum
time necessary to gain benefits.

3. _____ When muscle fibers undergo training, an increase
in the oxygen system enzymes can result.

4. _____ Stress fractures are uncommon in bones of highly
trained aerobic students.

5. _____ The principle of specificity implies that a variety
of cardiovascular work can specifically work the
same muscles, joints and ligaments.

6. _____ Placing the thumb over an artery in the wrist is
not recommended.

7. _____ There is more than one method to determine
maximal heart rate.

8. _____ Karvonen's formula is a reliable yet subjective
method of assigning workload for aerobic training.

III. Fill-In Questions

Read each statement carefully and fill in the space provided
with the best response.

1. Define the principle of reversibility. _____

_____

_____

2. List the four training principles. _____

_____

_____

3. What contributes to a lack of improvement in aerobic fitness despite consistent participation in an exercise program?

_____

_____

4. Define the term perceived exertion. _____

_____

_____

5. Explain Karvonen Heart Rate method. _____

_____

_____

IV. Clinical Discussions/Assignments

1. Discuss the training effects of cardiovascular exercise on heart, lungs, blood distribution, blood and body composition.
2. Explain the difference between endurance training and strength training, and describe two different exercise programs for each.

ANSWERS FOR CHAPTER SEVEN
I. Multiple Choice Questions
1. c - p.101-104
2. d - p.99-101
3. d - p.101
4. a - p.107
5. b - p.106
6. a - p.104
7. d - p.105-107
8. c - p.111
9. b - p.99
10. b - p.100

II. True or False Items
1. False - p.105
2. False - p.106
3. True - p.99
4. False - p.99
5. False - p.98
6. True - p.102
7. True - p.102
8. False - p.105

III. Fill-In Questions
1. If one stops participating in a regular physical activity program, all of the positive adaptations which have occured will reverse and eventually be lost. - p.109
2. Specificity, overload, variability and reversibility. - p.109
3. Lack of sleep, inadequate nutrition, another illness or health problem which may interfere with activity. - p.107
4. The total amount of exertion and physical fatigue that one perceives, combining all feelings of physical stress, effort and fatigue. - p.105
5. The method is based on the minimal threshold for training the cardiovascular system. Its calculation is as follows: Target Heart Rate Zone = Resting Heart Rate plus 70 to 80% of the difference between Maximum Heart Rate and Resting Heart Rate. - p.101

Chapter 8

Nutrition For Endurance and Training

U pon completion of this unit, you should have a basic knowledge of sports nutrition, hydration, carbohydrate loading, and optimal fuel sources.

I. Multiple Choice Questions

Read each question carefully and choose the best response. Circle your answer.

1. Prevention of muscle fatigue requires an adequate supply of muscle glycogen, the storage form of:
   a. protein   b. fat
   c. minerals   d. carbohydrates

2. The food recommendations for adults form the Basic Four Food Groups for minimum nutrient needs and contain approximately:
   a. 1000 calories   b. 1200 calories
   c. 1500 calories   d. 1800 calories

3. In order to replace exhausted muscle glycogen losses in 24 hours, a 120-pound active person's diet should include the following amounts of carbohydrates each day:
   a. 100-200 grams   b. 700-800 grams
   c. 1000 grams   d. 500-600 grams

4. Indications of low blood sugar would include all of the following EXCEPT:
   a. dizziness   b. paralysis
   c. confusion   d. partial blackout

5. The recommendation of 0.8-1.0 gram per kilogram of body weight will supply the average adult with a more than adequate supply of:
   a. carbohydrates   b. fat
   c. protein   d. minerals

6. Aerobic exercise burns this as a major fuel, and even lean marathon runners are well equipped to supply it from bodily storage areas:
   a. fat
   b. protein
   c. minerals
   d. carbohydrates

7. Treatment of the first stage of dehydration would include all of the following EXCEPT:
   a. Increase cold fluids by 1/2 cup every 15 minutes.
   b. Remove as much clothing as possible.
   c. Stop exercise.
   d. Rest in a warm environment.

8. Carbohydrate loading is a dietary procedure that includes all of the following EXCEPT:
   a. a set seven day exercise procedure.
   b. maximizing muscle glycogen storage.
   c. use of glucose or fructose drinks.
   d. a high carbohydrate diet (80% carbohydrate).

9. Guidelines for the pre-event meal plan include all of the following EXCEPT:
   a. avoid excessive intake of whole grain cereals and breads.
   b. decrease the fat content of the meal by avoiding margarines.
   c. decrease your water intake.
   d. avoid simple sugars.

10. The following statement is **not** true of sports drinks.
    a. they must stay in the stomach until diluted.
    b. they are the best fluid an athlete can drink.
    c. they can possibly hurt an athlete's performance.
    d. they should be diluted at least 50%.

II. True or False Items

Read each statement carefully. If correct, write TRUE on the line provided; if incorrect, write FALSE on the line provided.

1. _____ The demand for higher caloric intake due to energy expenditure in an exercise program can best be met by increasing the number of servings of food from the Basic Four Food Groups.

2. _____ Short spurts of intense exercise (anaerobic exercise) exclusively utilize glucose for energy while exercise of longer duration at low-to-moderate intensity (aerobic) burns approximately equal percentages of fat and glucose for the work.

3. __F__ Those engaged in more than two hours of continuous, strenuous workouts should consider the use
of carbonated soft beverages such as Coca Cola or
Pepsi to prevent low blood sugar.

4. __T__ Protein requirements are identical for the
untrained and trained athletic person.

5. __F__ Responding to thirst is a reliable guide to needs
during the profuse sweating stage of performance.

6. __T__ For effective treatment of heat exhaustion, stop
exercise, cool your environment and drink two cups
of water per pound of loss.

7. __F__ Carbohydrate loading is recommended before
short-term, high intensity competition of less than
four minutes.

8. __T__ During exercise, digestion of food will continue
slowly or not at all since the available blood
supply is shunted to the working muscles.

III. Fill-In Questions

Read each statement carefully and fill in the space provided
with the best response.

1. A high carbohydrate diet is one in which carbohydrates
account for approximately _____% of the calories
consumed each day.

2. Following performance, fluids should be taken as needed to
reinstate weight. _____ is the best fluid
to drink.

3. Low intensity, long duration aerobic exercise burns
_____ as a major fuel.

4. Conversion of carbohydrate particles into energy molecules
requires the cooperative effect of _____ vitamins.

5. A heavy meal must be consumed a minimum of _____
hours before exercise.

IV. Clinical Discussions/Assignments

1. A client who plans to run in a marathon wants to carbohydrate load as preparation for the race. Outline two 7-day
diet and exercise plans—one according to Technique B.

2. A participant in your aerobics class shows definite signs of
heat exhaustion. Describe appropriate treatment using as
much detail as possible.

ANSWERS FOR CHAPTER EIGHT

I.   Multiple Choice Questions

1. d - p.113
2. b - p.113
3. d - p.114
4. b - p.115
5. c - p.115
6. a - p.115
7. d - p.116
8. c - p.117
9. c - p.121
10. b - p.116

II.   True or False Items

1. True - p.113
2. True - p.114
3. False - p.115
4. True - p.115
5. False - p.115
6. True - p.116
7. False - p.118
8. True - p.118

III.   Fill-In Questions

1. 55% - p.114
2. Plain, cold water - p.116
3. Fat - p.115
4. B - p.117
5. 2 - p.118

Chapter 9

Strength Training

U pon completion of this unit, you should understand the terms absolute and relative strength, the phases of strength development in terms of General Adaptation Syndrome, and the relationship between active rest and overtraining.

I. Multiple Choice Questions

Circle the best response.

1. There are many forms of strength. Absolute strength is usually defined as:
   a. the measurement of absolutes, such as total weight lifted.
   b. the measurement of strength as a value relative to body size and weight.
   c. the volume of low repetitions and high intensity.
   d. the volume of high repetitions and low intensity.
2. The purpose of active rest can be briefly described as which of the following:
   a. the art of cycling certain types of exercise systems to enhance training benefits.
   b. allowing the body to recover and prepare for another repetition.
   c. repeated participation in one endeavor, but varying psychological approach.
   d. remaining at a plateau stage of training.
3. Overload principle implies that we can:
   a. lift more weight and get stronger without any known limitations.

b. work against resistance until muscle failure results.

c. produce greater results with strength versus endurance.

d. produce a training effect when muscles are worked slightly beyond past performance.

4. Phase 3 of General Adaptation Syndrome is described as:

   a. temporary drop in performance level.

   b. peaking or ultimate performance.

   c. exhaustion from overtraining.

   d. recovery and rest.

5. Strength training is dependent upon which set of variables:

   a. specificity, variation, intensity, duration, and frequency.

   b. variation, specificity, intensity, duration, and muscle mass.

   c. specificity, intensity, duration, frequency, and efficiency.

   d. variation, intensity, duration, frequency, and rest.

II.   True or False Items

Read each statement carefully. If correct, write TRUE on the line provided; if incorrect, write FALSE.

1. _____ Hypertrophy is best achieved by lifting a high volume with a low intensity.

2. _____ Since periodization helps to achieve peak performance, it also produces overtraining.

3. _____ The use of wrist weights can contribute toward muscle definition.

4. _____ Increasing repetitions will lead to increased strength, but will do little for increasing muscular endurance.

5. _____ For athletes, weight training tasks are most efficient when they relate to the demands of the specific athletic task.

6. _____ For the average enthusiast, weight training should take place on consecutive days.

7. _____ Three sets of five repetitions with 80% RM qualifies as a workout for strength-power.

8. _____ Participation in a sport other than one in which the athlete regularly performs is considered active rest.

III.   Fill-In Questions

Read each statement and fill in the space with the best response.

1. Define the three stages of General Adaptation Syndrome.

_____

_____

2. Explain how the use of limb weights can be considered
   resistance training despite their very light weight.

_____

_____

ANSWERS FOR CHAPTER NINE

I.   Multiple Choice Questions

1. a - p. 123
2. b - p. 126
3. d - p. 124
4. c - p. 124
5. a - p. 124

II.   True or False Items

1. True - p. 125
2. False - p. 125
3. True - p. 126
4. False - p. 126
5. True - p. 126
6. False - p. 126
7. False - p. 125
8. True - p. 125

III.   Fill-In Questions

1. 1) reaction to the stimulus; 2) physiological and biomechanical changes in response to the stimulus; and 3) stress accumulates to the point of exhaustion of the body. - p. 124
2. Since the theory of specificity applies in all resistance training, limb weights that manage to overload the system through a high number of repetitions, despite a low intensity, may work towards muscle definition, and specific muscle endurance, as well as greater caloric burn. - p. 126

Chapter 10

Flexibility

Upon completion of this unit, you should understand the contractile properties of muscles, tendons and ligaments, and the difference between ballistic and static stretching techniques.

I. Multiple Choice Questions

Circle the best response.

1. Allowing the stretch to occur along a longitudinal line with the direction of muscle fibers produces:
   a. inhibitory response by the Golgi Tendon Organs.
   b. complete excitation of all muscle fibers.
   c. increase in core temperature during warm-up.
   d. eventual collagen fiber breakdown.

2. Flexibility can be dependent on a number of factors. Among them are which of the following:
   a. sex
   b. age
   c. temperature
   d. all of the above

3. The minimum length of time necessary to affect the GTOs is:
   a. 10 seconds
   b. 20 seconds
   c. 60 seconds
   d. 2 minutes

4. Muscle soreness after an exercise session is attributed to many causes. Prime among them is:

       a. overstretching

       b. incomplete relaxation leading to spasm and soreness

       c. GTOs never were activated

       d. none of the above

   5. An example of common muscle imbalance in regard to flexibility would be which of the following:

       a. tight brachialis, overstretched deltoid

       b. tight quadriceps, overstretched erector spinae

       c. tight soleus, overstretched iliopsoas

       d. tight hamstring, overstretched quadriceps

II. True and False Items

Read each statement carefully. If correct, write TRUE on the line provided; if incorrect, write FALSE.

1. _____ Static stretching is more effective than ballistic stretching.

2. _____ Static stretching is responsible for increased core temperature during warm-up.

3. _____ Sports such as tennis and basketball can prevent assymetrical dynamic imbalances.

III. Fill-In Questions

Read each statement and fill in the space provided with the best response.

1. Define the Golgi Tendon Organs and their role in stretching muscles. _____

_____

2. According to AFAA Guidelines, warm-up should consist of what activities?_____

_____

3. Discuss the specificity of flexibility and the need for stretching all muscles in the body. _____

_____

IV. Clinical Assignment

1. Design an entire 30-minute relaxation class that is based on static stretching. Include rhythmic limbering activities when appropriate.

ANSWERS FOR CHAPTER TEN

I.   Multiple Choice Questions

1. a - p.130
2. d - p.130-131
3. a - p.130
4. b - p.131
5. d - p.131

II.   True and False Items

1. True - p.130
2. False - p.130
3. False - p.131

III.   Fill-In Questions

1. Sensory receptors located at the musculo-tendon junctures which provide the muscle with a protective mechanism during stretching. After a demand to stretch has been initiated, the GTOs stimulate an inhibitory or relaxation response, once enough information has been received about the duration and the force of the stretch. - p.129-130.
2. Balanced combination of rhythmic limbering movements and static stretching. - p.130
3. Because flexibility is specific, stretching muscles in legs will have no effect on muscles in upper body. Stretching each muscle included in a vigorous workout will reduce soreness after the activity. - p.130

Chapter 11

Neuromuscular Power and Plyometrics

U pon completion of this unit, you should understand the principles of power, force, and the application of plyometric drills in the development of power.

I. Multiple Choice Questions

Circle the best response.

1. Plyometric exercises draw their force of opposing magnitude by utilizing which of the following:
   a. concentric contractile forces
   b. natural elastic components of muscle
   c. a only
   d. a & b
2. The art of overcoming the inertia of one's own body at an ever-increasing rate is known as:
   a. plyometrics
   b. acceleration
   c. contractile force
   d. amortization
3. Once an athlete drops below the peak speed of movement, he must concentrate on reversing a phenomena known as:
   a. bounding response
   b. amortization phase
   c. deceleration
   d. horizontal force development
4. Examples of plyometric drills include which of the following:

a. double leg take-offs
b. bounding
c. in-depth jumps
d. all of the above

5. Plyometrics relates to aerobic dance exercise in the following way:

a. the jumping required in a high impact class can directly benefit from plyometric training.
b. body control and neuromuscular reactivity can assist overall movement in a class.
c. anaerobic threshold can be challenged by plyometrics.
d. all of the above.

II. True or False Items

Read each statement carefully. If correct, write TRUE on the line provided; if incorrect, write FALSE on the line provided.

1. ___F___ When performing in-depth drills, one should jump to the ground, rather than step to the ground, in order to store kinetic energy.

2. ___F___ Stretch reflex should be avoided in plyometrics as in static stretching.

3. ___F___ Plyometrics are easy to perform exercises for any beginner.

4. ___T___ The time that lapses from ground contact to reversal of movement is known as the amortization phase.

5. ___T___ Plyometric training is accompanied by a great deal of mental preparation as the athlete learns to "touch and go" and thereby, reduces take-off time.

III. Fill-In Questions

Fill in the spaces provided with the best response.

1. Define power and relate it to force.
2. Explain the relationship of plyometrics to neuromuscular power.

ANSWERS FOR CHAPTER ELEVEN

I.   Multiple Choice Questions

1. d - p.133
2. b - p.135
3. c - p.135
4. d - p.133-135
5. d - p.136

II.   True or False Items

1. False - p.133
2. False - p.134
3. False - p.136
4. True - p.134
5. True - p.134

III.   Fill-In Questions

1. The ability to apply strength rapidly. Also, power is the ability to develop force over a set distance as rapidly as possible. - p.133
2. Learning to apply large amounts of force in short periods of time is best developed by plyometrics. Stored energy from the force of gravity is quickly responded to with a reaction of opposite magnitude, using the natural elastic components of the muscles to produce an explosive take-off. - p.133-134

Chapter 12

Applied Sports Psychology

U pon completion of this unit, you should be able to relate methods of mentally preparing for a physical performance to anxiety, motivation and goal setting.

I. Multiple Choice Questions

Read each question carefully and choose the best response. Circle your answer(s).

1. Leading an aerobic exercise class is certainly meaningful enough to produce a state of heightened arousal with anxiety and tension. This is particularly likely for:
   a. The less experienced instructor.
   b. one teaching a new class or level.
   c. one teaching at a new facility.
   d. all of the above.

2. The following are all excellent tools to deal with preactivity anxiety EXCEPT:
   a. the playing of soft music.
   b. the breathing practice.
   c. the opportunity to take a nap.
   d. the imagining of a favorite peaceful place.

3. The most effective techniques for mentally preparing for physical performance are: (Choose all that apply)
   a. imagery.
   b. mental rehearsal.
   c. aggression building.
   d. all of the above.

4. Examples of adaptive behavior include the following: (Choose all that apply)
   a. stopping the class momentarily.
   b. moving to a different sort of exercise.

c. taking a break.

d. cutting the class short.

5. Before a class gets under way, the leader has already thought through the entire session. The beginning segment is especially important because:

a. the instructor has an opportunity to meet the class.

b. it is the segment in which the class is most energetic.

c. the participants have a chance to see what exercise clothing is appropriate.

d. it sets the tone for the whole session.

6. The thoughtful instructor has planned the sequence of events to ensure all of the following EXCEPT:

a. the timing is right.

b. the music is set at an adequate volume.

c. the transitions are correct.

d. the correct level of energy is maintained.

7. Music utilized to set the tempo is important to the success of aerobic exercise classes. Music allows:

a. the instructor to monitor the continuity of his or her sequence at anytime without reference to clocks or notes.

b. the instructor freedom to vary the tempo within each measure.

c. the instructor to lead a class without any preparation. He or she merely relies on the chosen music to guide his or her movements.

d. none of the above.

8. Each class should be brought to a distinct ending called "closure." Closure can be achieved by:

a. a cool down routine.

b. relaxation exercises.

c. announcements.

d. all of the above.

9. From time to time, as a learning experience, one needs to use the results of leading classes. We can review, evaluate, and learn from our performance by: (Choose all that apply)

a. studying the negative aspects of our performances.

b. setting difficult-to-reach goals for our next class.

c. using analysis evaluation.

d. employing constructive criticism.

10. The major internal causative factors of success are: (Choose all that apply)

a. obsession   b. ability

c. effort   d. all of the above

II. True or False Items

Read each statement carefully. If correct, write TRUE on the line provided; if incorrect, write FALSE on the line provided.

1. ___T___ The mental approach to physical performance is equally as important as the physical activity itself.
2. ___F___ Preactivity anxiety is limited to less-experienced instructors.
3. ___F___ There is a very definite need for deliberate cognitive intervention on the part of the instructor during the exercise session.
4. ___T___ The instructor is largely responsible for motivating the participants.
5. ___F___ Motivation based upon threats of termination or desire for monetary regard is intrinsic motivation.
6. ___F___ When an instructor has more than one class to lead in one day, he or she should sustain the arousal and intensity level.
7. ___T___ We are able to increase our accomplishments markedly by applying more effort.

III. Fill-In Questions

Read each statement carefully and fill in the space provided with the best responses.

1. Explain how normal arousal can be helpful. _____

_____

2. Describe how the the use of imagery and mental rehearsal are effective techniques for mentally preparing for physical performance. _____

_____

3. The drive toward self-fulfillment and competence is _____ motivation.

4. _____ is a tangible measure of success.

5. Explain how objective assessment of performance and constructive criticism of one's efforts are the mark of the professional instructor. _____

_____

IV. Clinical Discussions/Assignments

1. Using the technique of imagery, list at least 5 complications or difficulties that may occur in an upcoming workout session. For each problem, describe in detail how you, the instructor, would respond in order to ensure that the goals of the workout are attained.
2. Research and explain Benson's relaxation response. Develop and describe a program of practice that an individual could employ in order to become adept at using this technique effectively.

ANSWERS FOR CHAPTER TWELVE

I. Multiple Choice Questions

1. d   - p.138
2. c   - p.138
3. a,b - p.139
4. b,c - p.139
5. d   - p.139
6. b   - p.140
7. a   - p.140
8. d   - p.140
9. c,d - p.140
10. b,c - p.141

II. True or False Items

1. True - p.137
2. False - p.138
3. False - p.139
4. True - p.140
5. False - p.140
6. False - p.140
7. True - p.141

III. Fill-In Questions

1. Normal arousal permits us to really concentrate and focus upon the tasks ahead and then provide us with a surge of energy to accomplish these tasks. - p.138
2. By the use of imagery, we are able to construct the conditions of the upcoming workout allowing us to clarify expectations and foresee complications. The mental rehearsal allows us to reinforce a method of technical approach by repeated mental practice of an action or a sequence of actions. - p.139
3. Intrinsic. - p.140
4. Improvement. - p.140
5. Analysis of performance and efforts can provide appropriate goals and indicate changes that will create improvement in the future. - p.140-141

Chapter 13

Sports Injury Prevention

U pon completion of this unit, you should have an understanding of the factors which influence injury prevention, fatigue and overstress, as well as the principles of body mechanics and proper alignment.

I. Multiple Choice Questions

Circle the best response.

1. Ways in which to dissipate shock in an aerobics class are the following:
   a. switching from high-impact to low-impact moves.
   b. proper aerobic footwear designed to take the stress of a high-impact load.
   c. exercise on floors that "give" such as suspended wood or resilient mats.
   d. all of the above.

2. According to AFAA guidelines, aerobic instructors should limit their classes to:
   a. 2 per day, 13 per week.
   b. 3 per day, 10 per week.
   c. 3 per day, 12 per week.
   d. 2 per day, 12 per week.

3. Signs of an impending injury can include:
   a. numbness, tingling.
   b. slight loss of motion in the joints.
   c. general fatigue.
   d. any of the above.

4. For deconditioned beginning participants in an aerobic program, classes should be limited to:
   a. 90-minute session
   b. 45-minute session
   c. 30-minute session
   d. 60-minute session
5. A common problem resulting from standing with hyperextended knees is the following:
   a. excessive curve in the lower back with accompanying discomfort.
   b. weakening of the abdominal muscles.
   c. overstretching of the anterior tibialis.
   d. none of the above.
6. Which of the following exercises should be avoided in a beginning exercise class?
   a. plow.
   b. quadricep rock.
   c. donkey kicks.
   d. all of the above.

II.   True or False Items

Read each statement carefully. If correct, write TRUE on the line provided; if incorrect, write FALSE.

1. ___F___ Stretching is always accompanied by some pain.
2. ___F___ Only the well-trained body cannot be pushed to a point of fatigue and breakdown.
3. ___F___ The principle of overload has no bearing in an aerobics class since an instructor should never push her participants to a point of fatigue.
4. ___F___ Adequate warm-up and cooldown, although important, are not related to injury prevention.
5. ___T___ There is a tendency for muscles to shorten slightly after a period of injury and healing.
6. ___F___ Ballistic stretching is only recommended during the warm-up phase of an aerobics class.

III.   Fill-In Questions

Fill in the space provided with the best response.

1. Give at least three reasons why static stretching should be used during warm-up and cooldown. _____

_____

_____

2. Why is it important to avoid full squats in an aerobics class?

_____

_____

3. Describe proper body position for standing exercises.

_____

_____

4. Describe a safe way to perform a semi-squat. _____

_____

_____

IV. Clinical Discussion/Assignment

1. Perform a typical floor exercise such as side-lying leg lifts. Ask yourself AFAA's Five Questions while performing the exercise, and evaluate the response.
   a. What is the purpose of this exercise: stretching, strengthening, etc?
   b. Am I really doing that?
   c. Is the lower back protected and are there any major stress points?
   d. Am I isolating the muscle or muscle group that I'm intending to work?
   e. For whom is this exercise appropriate or inappropriate?

ANSWERS FOR CHAPTER THIRTEEN

I.　Multiple Choice Questions

1. d - p.146
2. c - p.144
3. d - p.144
4. c - p.144
5. a - p.144
6. d - p.289

II.　True or False Items

1. False - p.143
2. False - p.143
3. False - p.144
4. False - p.143
5. True - p.145
6. False - p.145

III.　Fill-In Questions

1. 1) There is less danger of muscle tissue damage; 2) The energy requirement is less; and 3) There is prevention or relief from muscular distress and soreness. - p.145
2. Full squats, particularly forceful, bouncing squats are harmful to knee ligaments. An overstretched ligament can lead to patellar instability and chronic knee problems. - p.144
3. Body held erect, shoulders level and back, abdominals held in firmly, knees soft, not hyperextended, and buttocks tucked under. - p.144
4. Never bring the hips below the level of the knees. Start with a good base of support, feet shoulder-width apart. With the body weight centered so that a straight line can be drawn through the center of the knees over the toes, both feet and toes should be slightly out to the side. - p.144

   Even this modified plie requires quadricep strength, so it is not recommended for deconditioned beginners.

Chapter 14

Common Aerobic Injuries

U pon completion of this unit, you should understand causes and common types of injuries, along with methods of prevention and first aid treatment.

I.   Multiple Choice Questions

Circle the best response.

1. Pain from an acute injury that is accompanied by swelling and loss of function should have the following assessment:
   a. Complete rest of limb, with professional evaluation within 1-3 days.
   b. Decrease in intensity of activity, with evaluation within 10-14 days.
   c. Aspirin, icing and altered regimen of stretching and strengthening.
   d. Alternation of icing and wrapping for 14 days.
2. Low back pain can be caused by many factors. Common among these is:
   a. weak abdominal muscles.
   b. tight hamstrings.
   c. improper body mechanics.
   d. any of the above.
3. In a compartment syndrome injury, the following signs are indicative of a problem in the anterior compartment:
   a. warmth, swelling, redness over the medial malleolus.
   b. tingling over the dorsum of the foot.

    c. pronation over ankle joint.

    d. tight calf muscles.

4. Excessive pronation of the ankle joint can lead to:

    a. posterior tibial tendinitis.

    b. pain in the posteriomedial border.

    c. overuse injuries in the tibial muscle.

    d. all of the above.

5. Identify three common injuries of the foot:

    a. plantar fasciitis, tendinitis and stress fractures.

    b. plantar fasciitis, metatarsalgia, and tensor latae fascia strain.

    c. metatarsalgia, stress fractures and posterior compartment syndrome.

    d. metatarsalgia, tendinitis, and anterior cruciate ligament tears.

6. Heel spurs can cause a burning pain in the front part of the heel. This condition is also known as:

    a. achilles tendinitis

    b. metatarsalgia

    c. stress fractures

    d. plantar fasciitis

7. An activity to perform during healing of a metatarsal stress fracture would be:

    a. swimming

    b. skating

    c. low impact aerobics

    d. jumping rope

8. A high-arched or cavus foot can lead to a painful condition in the foot known as:

    a. plantar fasciitis

    b. achilles tendinitis

    c. stress fracture

    d. metatarsalgia

9. A good rule of thumb to follow when returning from an injury is the following:

    a. allow approximately one week of rest for every week of disability.

    b. switch to another activity immediately.

    c. decrease the intensity of the activity and never stop.

    d. allow approximately two weeks of gradual increase in activity for every week of disability.

10. Certain anatomical malalignments may require that the instructor make the following recommendations to her student:

    a. Referral to a physician for examination prior to beginning aerobics.

    b. Remain at a beginner level until there is evidence of correction.

    c. Obtain orthotics to correct the limb position.

    d. Some pain is to be expected after activity with any malalignment.

II.   True or False Items

Read each statement carefully. If correct, write TRUE on the line provided; if incorrect, write FALSE.

1. _____ Overuse injuries are caused by repetitive impact and microtrauma together with an insufficient recovery period for healing between bouts of vigorous exercise.

2. _____ Overuse injuries are limited to soft tissue injury.

3. _____ For injury discomfort that continues beyond 14 days, re-application of RICE is recommended.

4. _____ Severe vasoconstriction without reversal results after icing an area for 20 minutes.

5. _____ A straight leg raise while sitting works the hip flexor muscles only.

6. _____ Squatting is used to strengthen patellar stability after an injury.

7. _____ Pain free range of motion is a reliable sign of full recovery after an injury.

8. _____ A stress fracture in the hip or femur bone is a common aerobics injury that requires RICE and a slow return to class.

III.   Fill-In Questions

Fill in the space provided with the best response.

1. Define RICE, and discuss its appropriate use. _____

_____

_____

2. Explain the factors that contribute to low back pain. _____

_____

_____

3. What are the types of treatments following an application of RICE? _____

_____

IV.   Clinical Discussions/Assignments

1. Explain a typical sequence of events during a knee ligament sprain or cartilage injury. Suggest types of exercise movements that would avoid knee sprains and injuries.

ANSWERS FOR CHAPTER FOURTEEN

I. Multiple Choice Questions

1. a - p.147
2. d - p.153
3. b - p.151
4. d - p.150-153
5. a - p.153
6. d - p.149
7. a - p.149
8. d - p.148
9. d - p.155
10. a - p.152

II. True or False Items

1. True - p.147
2. False - p.147
3. False - p.148
4. False - p.154
5. False - p.153
6. False - p.152
7. True - p.152
8. False - p.153

III. Fill-In Questions

1. Rest, Ice, Compression and Elevation—the four steps for early treatment of an acute injury. - p.154-155
2. Tight hamstrings, weak abdominal muscles, weak back extensor muscles, excessive or diminished lumbar curve, poor posture, and use of improper body mechanics. - p.153
3. Depending on the type of injury, and recommendations of a professional athletic trainer or physician, other treatment might include: gentle stretching and strengthening exercises, decrease in activity to painfree level, substitution of other activities, temporary cessation of activity or use of aspirin. - p.147

Part B

Developing an Aerobic Program

Chapter 1

Fitness Testing and Exercise Prescription

U pon completion, you should be able to describe various methods of fitness assessments, give an estimate of fitness capacity based on test data, and understand the basics of exercise screening.

I. Multiple Choice Questions

Read each question carefully and choose the best response. Circle your answer.

1. Functional capacity of an unfit individual differs from the functional capacity of a fit individual in that the unfit's capacity is:
   a. roughly twice as high due to the inverse ratio.
   b. about the same, since it is functional, not maximal.
   c. the same as the target heart rate.
   d. roughly half the capacity of the fit individual.

2. Methods of exercise testing include:
   a. standardized workload.
   b. graded ergometer test.
   c. treadmill test.
   d. all of the above.

3. Exercise stress tests, according to AFAA Standards and Guidelines, are recommended for:
   a. participants over 30 who have not had a check-up in the last year.
   b. participants ages 35 and over.
   c. participants ages 35 and over only if they have two or more risk factors.
   d. anyone new to vigorous exercise.

4. Heart rate and blood pressure are measured during stress tests. They are used to estimate which of the following:
   a. functional aerobic capacity.

      b. maximal oxygen consumption.

      c. basal metabolic rate.

      d. cardiovascular response to graded workloads.

  5. Isokinetic testing and training equipment such as the Cybex machine can be used to measure which of the following:

      a. assess major muscle strength.

      b. identify the strength imbalances between opposing muscle groups.

      c. assess the application of maximal force through entire range of motion.

      d. all of the above.

  6. Protocol for a common step test is as follows:

      a. 12" step, rate of 24 steps/minute, 3 minute test.

      b. 10" step, rate of 20 steps/minute, 3 minute test.

      c. 10" step, rate of 24 steps/minute, 2 minute test.

      d. 12" step, rate of 20 steps/minute, 3 minute test.

  7. Examples of a fitness evaluation for a specific muscle's endurance which require no equipment are which of the following:

      a. one and a half mile run.

      b. 1 RM determination.

      c. sit-ups, push-ups.

      d. some equipment is always needed.

  8. Careful screening is advisable before allowing someone to perform fitness tests due to which of the following:

      a. aggravation of pre-existing medical conditions.

      b. tests should be done in hospital setting only.

      c. tests should be administered freely; risks are minimal.

      d. body fat must be decreased in order to perform most tests.

II. True or False Items

Read each statement carefully. If correct, write TRUE on the line provided; if incorrect, write FALSE on the line provided.

  1. __T__ Someone with a high aerobic capacity will attain high workloads before reaching a target heart rate.

  2. __F__ Heart recovery tests measure the speed at which the heart rate rises during a set amount of time.

  3. __F__ All exercise stress tests are medical diagnostic tests designed to detect the presence of cardiovascular disease.

4. _F___ The recovery heart rate is as good a predictor of aerobic capacity as the heart rate actually measured during aerobics.

5. _____ 1 RM is equal to one repetition at maximal effort.

6. _____ Exercise tests that are graded can either measure oxygen consumption directly or indirectly.

III.   Fill-In Questions

Read each statement carefully and fill in the space provided with the best response.

1. The 1-1/2 mile run is undesirable as a means of fitness testing a 60-year-old beginner for the following reason: _____

   _____

   _____

2. Define muscular endurance:_____

3. Define muscle strength. _____

   _____

4. Explain the two steps necessary to perform before beginning an exercise program. _____

   _____

5. An exercise stress test is preferable to an age-related chart for determining THR for the following reason: _____

   _____

   _____

IV.   Clinical Discussions/Assignments

1. A 65-year-old woman wants to begin aerobics and enter your class. At 5'3", she weighs 165. She tells you her goal is weight loss. Describe your recommendations for beginning an exercise program.

2. A 55-year-old beginner reaches a heart rate of only 112 during your aerobics class. Explain the possible causes for this heart rate response, and discuss your recommendations to the client.

ANSWERS FOR CHAPTER ONE

I. Multiple Choice Questions

1. d - p.165
2. d - p.161
3. b - p.viii
4. d - p.161
5. d - p.163
6. a - p.162
7. c - p.163
8. a - p.163

II. True or False Items

1. True - p.161
2. False - p.162
3. False - p.161
4. False - p.162
5. True - p.163
6. True - p.160

III. Fill-In Questions

1. It subjects the participant to maximal exercise without monitoring any variables or signs of intolerance. - p.162
2. The ability of the muscle or muscle group to perform repeating contractions. - p.162
3. Maximal force that can be generated by a muscle or group of muscles. - p.162
4. 1) evaluate the capacity for exercise; 2) design a program suited to fitness level, health condition and activity interests. - p.159
5. The actual measurement of functional capacity is preferable to an estimated table for individuals due to the wide variability for maximum heart rate. - p.159

Chapter 2

Class Design and Conduct

U pon completion, you should be able to design and describe an effective exercise class that includes proper pre-class instructions and rationale for essential phases of a workout.

I.   Multiple Choice Questions

Read each question carefully and choose the best response.

1. The design and content of a one-hour aerobic exercise class includes all of the following EXCEPT:
   a. warm-up   b. abdominal work
   c. cooldown   d. none of the above
2. The warm-up period should consist of the following. Choose two:
   a. static stretching   b. aerobic exercise
   c. limbering exercises   d. ballistic movement
3. Strong, firm muscles in the arms, chest, and shoulders are important to women because they:
   a. help maintain correct body alignment.
   b. provide natural support for the breasts.
   c. help maintain correct posture.
   d. all of the above.
4. An aerobically fit cardiovascular system will allow the individual to:
   a. work longer and more vigorously.
   b. sleep more soundly.
   c. run faster.
   d. all of the above.
5. Jogging on your toes is dangerous because: (Choose two)
   a. it shortens the calf muscles.
   b. it damages the bones in the toes.
   c. it shortens the achilles tendon.

    d. it decreases the effect of the workout.
6. Heart rates should be taken at which of the following points during the workout? (Choose two)
    a. just after the warm-up.
    b. before the cooldown.
    c. 5 minutes into the cooldown.
    d. 5 minutes into the aerobic workout.
7. Strong abdominal muscles will:
    a. provide a cosmetically pleasing effect.
    b. support the trunk.
    c. prevent lower back pain.
    d. all of the above.
8. The wonderful part about stretching at the end of class is:
    a. the relaxed feeling it creates.
    b. the number of calories burned.
    c. the amount of muscle building it provides.
    d. none of the above.
9. It is advisable for the following populations to take a final heart rate count after final cooldown and stretching: (Choose two)
    a. those with a slower than average recovery time.
    b. those with risk factors.
    c. older participants.
    d. all of those who appear tired.
10. Saunas, hot tubs, and hot showers should be avoided immediately following exercise because:
    a. fatigue is too great.
    b. heat causes blood vessels to dilate.
    c. heat creates a false sense of flexibility.
    d. all of the above.

II.   True or False Items.

Read each statement carefully. If correct, write TRUE on the line provided; if incorrect, write FALSE on the line provided.

1. _____ Class should always begin with a warm-up period.
2. _____ The warm-up period should last a minimum of 4-6 minutes.
3. _____ 25 side-lying leg lifts properly executed can do more for body toning of the outer thigh than 40 of them in the wrong position.
4. _____ The speed at which exercises are performed is not important.

5. _F_ In order to improve one's fitness level, 3 times a week is considered the optimum number of aerobic workouts.

6. _T_ Participants should work at a level where they could converse, but be required to use short sentences.

7. _F_ Standing waist exercises are highly effective.

8. _T_ Exercises for the buttocks can be potentially dangerous to the lower back if performed incorrectly.

9. _F_ The least effective exercises for strengthening abdominals are abdominal curls.

10. _T_ Static stretching is most effective at the end of your class.

III. Fill-In Questions

Read each statement carefully and fill in the space provided with the best response.

1. Explain why the warm-up period is crucial to a successful workout. _____

_____

2. Give some examples of rhythmic limbering. _____

_____

_____

3. Explain the benefits of aerobic exercises. _____

_____

_____

4. Describe how to take/monitor a heart rate. _____

_____

_____

5. Explain what happens when one performs peak movements continuously. _____

_____

IV. Clinical Discussions/Assignments

1. Design a plan for a one-hour aerobic exercise class that a new instructor can easily follow. Divide your class structure into appropriate categories spanning all necessary phases of

an aerobic workout. Develop the content of your class by discussing the following:

a. specific exercises to be used,
b. purpose of the exercises,
c. which muscles are being used,
d. time allotment,
e. variations and transitions,
f. injury prevention,
g. risk factors,
h. adaptive techniques.

2. An ambitious student in your aerobics class asks for a customized program of exercises that she can perform at home on days when the class does not meet. Particular areas of concern to this student are the waist, thighs and abdomen. Design a 15-minute exercise that concentrates on these areas.

ANSWERS FOR CHAPTER TWO

I. Multiple Choice Questions

1. d - p.169
2. a,c - p.172
3. d - p.173-174
4. a - p.175
5. a,c - p.176
6. b,d - p.177
7. d - p.183
8. a - p.184
9. a,b - p.185
10. b - p.185

II. True or False Items

1. True - p.171
2. True - p.172
3. True - p.169
4. False - p.175
5. False - p.175
6. True - p.178
7. False - p.180
8. True - p.182
9. False - p.183
10. True - p.184

III. Fill-In Questions

1. It will prepare the body for more vigorous exercise by increasing the flexibility of muscles, tendon, and ligaments, thus allowing for a full range of motion while minimizing the possibility of injury. - p.172
2. Small arm circles, leg circles, knee lifts, high reaches, and small kicks. - p.173
3. Aerobic exercises train the heart, lungs, and cardiovascular system to process and deliver oxygen quickly and efficiently to every part of the body. As the heart muscle becomes stronger and more efficient, it is able to pump more blood with each stroke and in fewer strokes, thus facilitating the rapid transport of oxygen to all parts of the body. - p.175
4. The pulse is located in the wrist below the thumb. Student should keep walking while taking heart rate. Count the pulses for 10 seconds and multiply by 6. - p.177

5. Peak movements require anaerobic metabolism, which produces lactic acid. Once lactic acid production is initiated, levels will rise and cause exhaustion within only a few minutes. - p.178

Chapter 3

Body Shaping

Upon completion of this unit, you should have a basic understanding of the principles of weight training as they relate to body contouring, and be able to provide a client with a body shaping plan for his/her particular somatotype.

I. Multiple Choice Questions

Read each question carefully and choose the best response.

1. Weight training by females will:
   a. develop massive muscles.
   b. increase muscle tissue.
   c. add shape and definition to the figure.
   d. both b and c.
2. Sweating pounds off can lead to:
   a. significant weight loss.
   b. pneumonia.
   c. dehydration.
   d. all of the above.
3. In response to dieting, your body: (Choose two)
   a. learns to exist on fewer calories.
   b. converts calories.
   c. burns fat.
   d. reduces the need to burn calories.
4. Body composition refers to:
   a. the ratio of fat and lean body mass.
   b. the number of red blood cells.
   c. the vital body organs.
   d. none of the above.
5. Aerobic exercise:
   a. improves the cardiovascular and respiratory systems.
   b. increases the individual's work capacity.
   c. burns fat as fuel.
   d. all of the above.

6. When striving for consistency, you should work out with a partner. A partner can be a real asset as:
   a. a motivator.
   b. a source of competition.
   c. an outlet for frustration.
   d. all of the above.
7. To decrease the possibility of overtraining:
   a. exercise for short periods only.
   b. allow periods of rest in your training regimen.
   c. follow an expert's program exactly.
   d. stop only when it becomes necessary for you to strain.
8. The fundamental components to your success in training are: (Choose two)
   a. regularity.
   b. a healthy diet.
   c. a clear plan for achievement.
   d. a difficult program.
9. Goals are meant to be:
   a. an incentive.
   b. the last word.
   c. far beyond one's normal grasp.
   d. none of the above.
10. The best way to reward yourself after a good workout is:
    a. a favorite sweet.
    b. to do something you enjoy.
    c. to not exercise for several days.
    d. none of the above.

II. True or False Items

Read each statement carefully. If correct, write TRUE on the line provided; if incorrect, write FALSE on the line provided.

1. _____ Aerobics is the only exercise you need.
2. _____ Strengthening exercise will not help spot reducing.
3. _____ It is generally considered desirable for an adult male to have 8%-11% fat.
4. _____ Although it's not optimal, one could lose fat by dieting.
5. _____ Strength training only maintains muscle tissue.
6. _____ There is no one successful method of training.
7. _____ Proper preparation lends itself to a more consistent training.

8. ___F___ Goals should not be changed until the original ones
have been met.
9. ___F___ If you feel tired, the best thing to do is cancel your
exercise immediately.
10. ___T___ Strength contributes significantly to overall fitness.

III. Fill-In Questions

Read each statement carefully and fill in the space provided
with the best responses.

1. List and define the three general body types. _____

_____

_____

2. Define fat. _____

_____

3. Define basal metabolic rate (BMR). _____

_____

4. Explain the importance of flexibility. _____

_____

_____

5. List the three basic methods to increase the training intensity
and effects of an exercise. _____

_____

IV. Clinical Discussions/Assignments

1. A balanced program of aerobics, strength training and flexibility exercises are essential for successful body shaping.
Take the first step in designing such a program for a client
by compiling a list consisting of one basic exercise per body
part. For each exercise, provide detailed, accurate instructions that your client will be able to follow easily.
2. Keep a training diary that charts your workouts for one
month. Include data regarding aerobic exercise, strength
and flexibility exercises, length of workouts, time of day,
your mood, and your food intake. As the month progresses,
notice the patterns that emerge. Formulate as many conclu-
sions as you can that are based on these patterns and that
will help you to work out in a more efficient and productive
manner.

ANSWERS FOR CHAPTER THREE

I. Multiple Choice Questions

1. d - p.188
2. c - p.189
3. a,d - p.192
4. a - p.192
5. d - p.192
6. a - p.196
7. b - p.197
8. a,c - p.206
9. a - p.206
10. b - p.207

II. True or False Items

1. False - p.188
2. True - p.189
3. False - p.191
4. True - p.191
5. False - p.193
6. True - p.197
7. True - p.206
8. False - p.206
9. False - p.207
10. True - p.208

III. Fill-In Questions

1. mesomorph: predominance of muscle on the body.
   endomorph: primarily round, chubby build.
   ectomorph: appearance of a lean and thin body. - p.190
2. Fat is stored energy. - p.190
3. BMR is the body's system of generating heat from calories consumed in order to function properly and meet the demands of a 24 hour period. - p.191
4. Flexibility is needed to move the body and its parts through a wide range of motion without undue stress to the muscle attachments or anatomical structure. - p.192
5. 1) Performing a greater number of repetitions with a specific weight; 2) increasing the weight and performing a specific number of repetitions; 3) doing an established number of sets and repetitions with a specific weight, using a shorter rest interval. - p.195

Chapter 4

Motivation and Habit Training

Upon completion of this unit, you should be able to develop a strategy for maximizing the motivation of all members in your class, and for assisting them in their attainment of positive health habits.

I. Multiple Choice Questions

Read each question carefully and choose the best response. Circle your answer.

1. Which of the following sensations tell you to stop exercising?
   a. modest discomfort (e.g., dry mouth, labored breathing).
   b. muscle soreness.
   c. pain.
   d. stiffness.
2. If a participant misses two weeks of class, it is best to:
   a. advise him to curtail exercise.
   b. advise him to drop back one level of intensity.
   c. instruct him to pick up at the same level when rejoining the class.
   d. none of the above.
3. Which of the following statements is not correct:
   a. more people than ever are participating in exercise programs.
   b. the incidence of heart disease has decreased.
   c. nutritional habits are changing.
   d. more people than ever have started smoking.
4. Which of the following factors have an effect on the adherence to exercise programs:
   a. time.
   b. health awareness.
   c. previous athletic experience.
   d. attitude toward physical activity.

5. Essential facts about exercising include information on:
   a. flexibility.   b. weight loss.
   c. strength.   d. all of the above.
6. The best time to exercise without interruption is:
   a. morning.   b. afternoon.
   c. evening.   d. before bed.
7. If a participant is suffering from a minor illness, it is best for him to:
   a. exercise as usual.
   b. exercise more vigorously in order to sweat out germs.
   c. curtail exercise.
   d. stop exercising for a minimum of a week.
8. How long should each participant commit himself for at the outset?
   a. two weeks.   b. six weeks.
   c. one month.   d. one year.
9. Which technique has the most motivating effect on a program participant?
   a. weighing in.
   b. shopping for new clothes.
   c. charting progress of measurements
   d. none of the above.
10. Habits are established by:
   a. cultural values.
   b. the repetition of behavior.
   c. societal expectations.
   d. none of the above.

II. True or False Items

Read each statement carefully. If correct, write TRUE on the line provided; if incorrect, write FALSE on the line provided.

1. ___T___ More than 30 million people have stopped smoking.
2. ___T___ Developed Western countries have the highest incidence of cardiovascular disease in the world.
3. ___F___ More than 80% of adults in the United States are overweight.
4. ___T___ 30%-50% of individuals who start an exercise program will drop out within the first ten weeks.
5. ___T___ Muscle soreness and stiffness is normal after a workout.

6. _____ F _____ A person's attitude toward physical activity has a significant effect on adherence to exercise programs.

7. _____ F _____ Research indicates that attrition is less common among those who exercise in the evening.

8. _____ T _____ Owing to changes in body composition brought about through exercise, body weight can be misleading.

9. _____ F _____ Regular aerobic exercise program participation should lead to a reduction in resting heart rate of two beats per minute for each two weeks during the first 16-20 weeks of the program.

10. _____ T _____ In order for an exercise program to become habit, it must be enjoyable.

III. Fill-In Questions

Read each statement carefully and fill in the space provided with the best response.

1. The scientific history of our species can be traced back _____ years.

2. What are the commonly reported reasons for the attrition of people from exercise programs? _____

_____

3. What are factors which do not appear to influence attrition from exercise programs? _____

_____

4. AFAA Standards recommend that an instructor teach no more than _____ classes per day.

5. In order to allow adequate time to experience the "training effect," encourage each participant in your exercise program to make at least a _____ commitment at the outset.

IV. Clinical Discussions/Assignments

1. A middle-aged woman who has led a mostly sedentary lifestyle has made a six-week commitment to participate in your exercise program. She needs encouragement, however, especially with regard to increased awareness of her changing physical fitness. Help her to chart her progress as a motivating technique. Include such variables as: girth measurements of waist and hips, resting heart rates and body weight.

ANSWERS FOR CHAPTER FOUR

I. Multiple Choice Questions

1. c - p.213
2. b - p.215
3. d - p.211
4. a - p.213
5. d - p.214
6. a - p.214
7. c - p.215
8. b - p.215
9. c - p.215
10. b - p.216

II. True or False Items

1. True - p.211
2. True - p.212
3. False - p.212
4. True - p.212
5. True - p.213
6. False - p.213
7. False - p.214
8. True - p.215
9. False - p.215
10. True - p.216

III. Fill-In Questions

1. 2 million. - p.211
2. Insufficient time, lack of self-discipline, lack of interest.
3. General health awareness, attitude toward physical activity, level of physical fitness, previous athletic experience, and socioeconomic status. - p.214
4. 3. - p.215
5. 6-week. - p.215

Part C

Professionalism and Aerobics

Professional Conduct/Certification/ Continuing Education

As a professional instructor, you should be able to address the areas of responsibility, types of credentials, and degree of training necessary for meeting nationally accepted standards in exercise instruction.

I. Multiple Choice Questions

Read each question carefully and choose the best response. Circle your answer.

1. Which term accurately describes the focus of aerobic instructors?
   - a. performance.
   - b. agility.
   - c. responsibility.
   - d. knowledge.

2. The degree of training and the type of credentials necessary for an aerobics instructor will vary according to:
   - a. the medical considerations of the students.
   - b. the fitness level of the students.
   - c. the physical considerations of the students.
   - d. all of the above.

3. As professional instructors, it is our role to do all of the following EXCEPT:
   - a. instruct.
   - b. treat injury.
   - c. motivate.
   - d. monitor.

4. The instructor's professionalism is exhibited through: (Choose two)
   - a. his or her commitment to improvement.
   - b. his or her visible level of fitness.
   - c. his or her presentation to students.
   - d. his or her medical knowledge.

5. The exercise experience for the consumer has been plagued by:
   - a. contradiction.
   - b. physical injury.
   - b. misinformation.
   - d. all of the above.

6. Certification can be the means by which the fitnesss industry designates the instructor as:
   a. qualified.   b. knowledgeable.
   c. professional.   d. all of the above.
7. Which of the following areas should be covered in the program curriculum?
   a. body composition.   b. CPR.
   c. basic anatomy.   d. all of the above.
8. The AFAA Certified aerobic instructor has demonstrated:
   a. a basic degree of competency.
   b. an understanding of most problems.
   c. a knowledge of how to treat any physical injury.
   d. all of the above.
9. Learning occurs in response to:
   a. dissatisfaction.   b. need.
   c. ignorance.   d. none of the above.
10. A plan for continuing education should include all of the following EXCEPT:
   a. at least one journal.
   b. classes taken in college.
   c. a mentor.
   d. organized classes.

II.   True or False Items

Read each statement carefully. If correct, write TRUE on the line provided; if incorrect, write FALSE on the line provided.

1. _____ It is the responsibility of the instructor to prescribe exercise treatment.
2. _____ It is the responsibility of the instructor to provide general information on everything from injury prevention to nutrition.
3. _____ Anyone 10 pounds overweight should not be instructing.
4. _____ Always wear clothing that's comfortable, dress for comfort not appearance.
5. _____ The instructor should be a source of healthy competition for the student.
6. _____ The fitness industry follows no governmental requirements or regulations.
7. _____ Certification should provide proof of knowledge and ability.

8. ___F___ A local club's certification is fine for an instructor facing the possibility of working in several different clubs.

9. ___T___ Continuing education is the cornerstone of a successful aerobics practice.

10. ___F___ AFAA Instructor Certification is valid for three years.

III. Fill-In Questions

Read each statement carefully and fill in the space provided with the best responses.

1. Define a profession. _____

_____

2. Define certification. _____

_____

3. AFAA believes the public is entitled two assurances. What are they? _____

_____

4. What is continuing education? _____

_____

5. List the factors that influence adult learning. _____

_____

_____

IV. Clinical Discussions/Assignments

1. In order to meet your responsibility as a fitness instructor to provide an appropriate training session, you must be fully qualified. The Aerobics and Fitness Association of America recommends instructor certification that requires a basic theoretical understanding and practical competency in certain areas. List these areas of basic curriculum and discuss the relevancy of each one to the fitness industry.

2. AFAA Instructor Certification is valid for two years. Within that period, a Certified Instructor must submit proof of continuing education in order to renew his or her certification. Explain in detail the AFAA Continuing Education requirements, answering the following questions:

a. How many hours of course work must be completed within the two year period?
b. What type of course is acceptable?
c. Are courses offering only practical experience acceptable?
d. Is any additional type of certification necessary?

ANSWERS FOR CHAPTERS 1-2-3

I.   Multiple Choice Questions

1. d - p.221
2. d - p.222
3. b - p.222
4. a,c - p.222-223
5. d - p.226
6. c - p.226
7. d - p.227
8. a - p.228
9. b - p.229
10. c - p.230

II.   True or False Items

1. False - p.222
2. True - p.222
3. False - p.222
4. False - p.223
5. False - p.223
6. True - p.226
7. True - p.226
8. False - p.227
9. True - p.230
10. False - p.231

III.   Fill-In Questions

1. A vocation or occupation which requires advanced or specialized training in the liberal arts or sciences. - p.225
2. Certification means that someone is validating the fulfillment of the requirements according to a certain standard. - p.226
3. 1) Safe and effective exercise instruction; 2) a standard by which to recognize the competency of the personnel directly administering an exercise class. - p.228
4. The process of lifelong learning. - p.229
5. A self-concept that is self-directed; a reservoir of life experiences; a readiness to learn because of a need to know, a problem-centered orientation to learning. - p.229

Part D

The Aerobics Business

Chapter 1

Starting Your Own Business

Fitness has a positive impact on life. Being a catalyst and helping other people discover that fact can be very challenging and exciting. In order to make your business succeed, however, you may have to work harder than you ever thought possible.

I. Multiple Choice Questions

Read each question carefully and choose the best response. Circle your answer.

1. In order to build a successful fitness business, there are five basic essentials you must have. Which of the following is **not** one of those essentials?
   a. a reasonable amount of intelligence.
   b. an enormous amount of energy.
   c. a Bachelor's degree in Physical Education.
   d. an adequate amount of capital.
   e. luck and good timing.
2. Generally, leaders in the fitness industry possess which of the following characteristics in common?
   a. The educational background required to meet the high standards in the fitness world.
   b. The confidence, flair, and finesse to teach.
   c. Certification or the willingness to take classes to become certified.
   d. The genetic luck to move well to music and to be extremely energetic.
   e. All of the above.

3. If you decide that you want to open your own fitness center, you will need to take all of the following steps EXCEPT:
 a. Set small, medium-sized, and big goals.
 b. Prepare with intelligence and be positive.
 c. Decide what the focus of your business will be.
 d. Tie-in with a franchise organization.
 e. Study the market in your town to calculate your chances for success.

4. Which of the following words of warning should you consider if you are planning a partnership? Choose two.
 a. Make a list of "business expectations" that covers even the smallest detail of the operation.
 b. Make sure that you and your prospective partner have approximately the same level of intelligence and ability with respect to the fitness field.
 c. Do not consider a partnership with someone unless you have enjoyed a long-standing, harmonious relationship with the person.
 d. Put everything down in writing, because money changes people.

5. In order to get your business started, you must have a reasonable amount of capital. Which of the following suggestions are effective ways to raise money?
 a. Talk to the local banks about personal loans or loans against your investments.
 b. Consider presenting a business plan and going after investors.
 c. Study the advantages and disadvantages of incorporation.
 d. Research how the Small Business Administration and various government agencies supply grants and low interest loans to small businesses.
 e. All of the above.

6. In addition to raising money, when running a business, it pays to find ways to *save money*. Which of the following are cost-cutting techniques? Choose two.
 a. Sponsor a fund raiser.
 b. Ask students to fill in as fitness instructors.
 c. Try bartering. Trade a month's free classes to a printing firm in exchange for the supplies you need such as business cards or stationery.
 d. Drastically reduce your advertising budget.

7. Owning your own business means **all** of the following EXCEPT:

   a. There is no one to tell you what to do or how to do it.

   b. There is freedom, but there are no established guidelines.

   c. Since you are the owner of the fitness business, it is not crucial that you be in peak condition.

   d. You may have to work seven days a week, especially in the beginning.

8. To help you and your business remain ahead of the competition, which of the following is helpful?

   a. Sign up for fitness seminars.

   b. Subscribe to professional journals.

   c. Go to motivational workshops.

   d. Network with other business and civic leaders.

   e. All of the above.

9. Some words of wisdom to remember if you own your own business are: Choose two.

   a. If you are also running a home, get some household help.

   b. Keep abreast of the constant changes in the fitness industry.

   c. Get so involved with your business that there is virtually nothing else in your life.

   d. Do not listen to criticism. This is a time for only positive feedback from others.

10. "Good timing" means:

    a. Being in the right place at the right time.

    b. Staying one step ahead-thinking up classes that someone else can't totally duplicate.

    c. Recognizing a trend and incorporating it into your business.

    d. Polishing your skills.

    e. All of the above.

II. True or False Items

Read each statement carefully. If correct, write TRUE on the line provided; if incorrect, write FALSE on the line provided.

1. _____ If you have a need to be in charge, you will probably enjoy owning your own business.

2. _____ When starting your own business you needn't spend time studying the competition.

3. _____ If you are going to have a partner, it is important that your idea of working hard agrees with his or her own.

4. _____ One area that a lot of new business owners neglect is the high cost of advertising.
5. _____ Putting all of your energy into your business is the only way to get started.
6. _____ It's wise to consider whether you will be able to stand the emotional tension associated with starting a new business.
7. _____ When times are tough, it's probably best to pull back and not try so hard.
8. _____ Most people still consider health and wellness to be a luxury item.

III. Fill-In Questions

Read each statement and fill in the space provided with the best response.

1. List at least three innovative ideas for exercise classes that will allow you to scoop the market and leave your competitors behind. _____

_____

2. As the owner of a fitness studio, sponsoring a fun-run for a civic group or helping to raise money for a specific city project is a good way to get free _____.

3. Name at least two topics that the U.S. Small Business Administration in Washington, D.C. offers training, counseling, and booklets on. _____

_____

4. What are two basic rules to remember when hiring people to work for you? _____

_____

5. Once you hire someone to work for you, it's important to create _____ to keep his or her motivation high.

IV. Clinical Discussions/Assignments

1. Pretend that you have just opened an exercise studio. Formulate an advertising campaign and develop a marketing plan that will help to bring your new business before the public eye.

ANSWERS FOR CHAPTER ONE

I.   Multiple Choice Questions

1. c - p.239
2. e - p.240
3. d - p.240
4. a,d - p.241
5. e - p.241
6. a,c - p.242
7. c - p.243
8. e - p.243
9. a,b -243
10. e - p.245

II.   True or False Items

1. True - p.240
2. False - p.241
3. True - p.241
4. True - p.242
5. False - p.243
6. True - p.243
7. False - p.244
8. True - p.244

III.   Fill-In Questions

1. A fit-to-ski program, a couples class, an exercise progam for tots, a senior or handicapped class. - p.241
2. Publicity. - p.242
3. Starting a small business, locating sources of financing, developing customers. - p.247
4. 1) Trust your instincts; 2) Check references. - p.246
5. Incentives. - p.246

Chapter 2

Legal Considerations

Upon completion of this unit, you should be able to describe these primary legal considerations: extent of liability, approval of program, qualifications of instructors, disclaimers and releases, and responsibility for negligence.

I. Multiple Choice Questions

Read each question carefully and choose the best response. Circle your answer.

1. The likelihood of injury is reduced when: (Choose two)
   a. the instructor is highly trained.
   b. the student stops exercising as soon as he feels a strain.
   c. the program is medically sound.
   d. the program largely consists of ballistic movements.
2. If a person proves he or she was injured while participating in an exercise class, he or she will:
   a. automatically win the lawsuit.
   b. automatically lose the lawsuit.
   c. be entitled to compensation.
   d. none of the above.
3. Whatever type of program your club follows, it is a good idea to have the basic program or exercises approved by:
   a. an instructor.
   b. sports medicine professionals.
   c. a cardiac specialist.
   d. all of the above.
4. An instructor training program should be documented by:
   a. a periodical.　　　　　　　b. a report by an expert.
   c. a manual.　　　　　　　　d. none of the above.
5. If an exercise club chooses not to obtain professional approval for the manual, it is best to:
   a. hide the manual.

    b. not allow the manual to be seen by the public.

    c. not compile a manual at all.

    d. none of the above.

6. To protect itself from liability an exercise club should:

    a. provide information handouts.

    b. have each participant sign a disclaimer.

    c. have each participant sign a release.

    d. all of the above.

7. In preparing such a release, it is advisable that which of the following be consulted:

    a. a sports medicine professional.

    b. an attorney.

    c. an accountant.

    d. a business manager.

8. In order to avoid being sued, an instructor should make it his or her business to:

    a. be properly trained.

    b. keep abreast of the latest developments and techniques in his or her training.

    c. update his or her training.

    d. all of the above.

9. Since the allegation that the instructor failed to properly warm up the class is so common, great care should be taken to:

    a. devise a program that is simple and that will not tax the participant.

    b. choreograph a safe and effective warm-up and stretching routine.

    c. see that each participant is following the program exactly.

    d. none of the above.

10. Before opening an exercise facility, one should: (Choose two)

    a. become familiar with local health club laws.

    b. find out about any pending legislation.

    c. sell memberships.

    d. post a bond with the state.

II.   True or False Items

Read each statement carefully. If correct, write TRUE on the line provided; if incorrect, write FALSE on the line provided.

1. _____ Anyone can file a lawsuit against anyone else.

2. _____ Aerobic exercise injury lawsuits can be prevented.

3. _____ The best protection against lawsuits is liability insurance.
4. _____ Liability insurance is a comprehensive policy.
5. _____ Instructors have no effect on the liability of an exercise studio.
6. _____ A copy of the instructor's manual should be kept in a central location, such as an office, at all times.
7. _____ Handouts provided for the student should outline the controversial exercises explicitly.
8. _____ A first-time guest to a club should be required to sign a disclaimer.
9. _____ In some states a release may be deemed invalid.

III.   Fill-In Questions

Read each question carefully and fill in the space provided with the best response.

1. List the measures which lessen the likelihood of injury and protect against liability. _____

_____

2. Why is liability insurance the best protection? _____

_____

_____

3. What should certification specifically describe? _____

_____

_____

4. What does a disclaimer do? _____

_____

5. Why is the indemnity agreement important? _____

_____

_____

ANSWERS FOR CHAPTER TWO

I. Multiple Choice Questions

1. a,c - p.249
2. d - p.249
3. b - p.250
4. c - p.251
5. c - p.251
6. d - p.252
7. b - p.253
8. d - p.253
9. b - p.253
10. a,b - p.256

II. True or False Items

1. True - p.249
2. False - p.249
3. True - p.250
4. False - p.250
5. False - p.251
6. True - p.251
7. False - p.252
8. True - p.252
9. True - p.253

III. Fill-In Questions

1. Purchasing liability insurance; developing a medically sound exercise program; hiring well qualified instructors; requiring the signing of a disclaimer and a release. - p.250
2. If an injured student sues the instructor or the studio, the insurance company will pay for and provide defense of the insured and pay any settlement or judgment fees up to the policy limit. - p.250
3. The instructor's training in basic areas essential to the teaching of exercise. - p.252
4. It disclaims any liability for negligence on the part of the exercise club or any of its employees. - p.252
5. Without it the instructor may be held personally responsible for all or a portion of the judgment and have to pay for an attorney to defend the case. - p.254

Chapter 3

Equipment For The Aerobics Business

Upon completion of this unit, you should be able to describe the difference between free weights and resistive weight equipment. You should also be familiar with the other types of equipment common to most fitness studios.

I.   Multiple Choice Questions

Read each question carefully and choose the best responses. Circle your answer.

1. While using a machine, clients:
    a. must be monitored closely.
    b. must follow a complicated, lengthy set of directions.
    c. need never be monitored.
    d. none of the above.

2. _____ continue to remain one of the most popular pieces of aerobic exercise equipment today.
    a. Rowing machines.
    b. Exercise cycles.
    c. Treadmills.
    d. Mini-trampolines.

3. Riding an exercise cycle:
    a. improves the cardiovascular system.
    b. tones the leg muscles.
    c. strengthens the leg muscles.
    d. all of the above.

4. Two things to look for on a noncomputerized exercise cycle are: (Choose two)
    a. a weighted flywheel.
    b. straps across the pedals.
    c. handlebar grips.
    d. a belt-braking resistance system.

5. Rowing machines have been incorporated into aerobics businesses mainly because:

a. they provide such a tremendous aerobic workout.
b. they have been so heavily promoted for home use.
c. they require so little skill and endurance.
d. all of the above.

6. Exercising on a treadmill provides the same cardiovascular and muscular benefits of:
a. running.
b. rowing
c. swimming.
d. cycling.

7. The least expensive hand-held weights are:
a. stainless steel.
b. teflon.
c. cast-iron.
d. none of the above.

8. Which of the following does not qualify as aerobic exercise:
a. swimming.
b. cross-country skiing.
c. running.
d. gymnastics.

9. The primary factor to consider when expanding your aerobics center with strength-training equipment is:
a. cost.
b. space.
c. popularity of given machine.
d. none of the above.

10. Currently, the two most popular pieces of equipment are: (Choose two)
a. machines that work the upper body.
b. abdominal machines.
c. lower body machines.
d. lower back machines.

II. True or False Items

Read each statement carefully. If correct, write TRUE on the line provided; if incorrect, write FALSE on the line provided.

1. ___F___ People restricted from rigorous exercise cannot use machines.

2. ___T___ The feedback that computerized machines provide is an important incentive to exercisers.

3. ___T___ The rowing machine is technically an aerobic fitness item.

4. _____ The use of free weights has been helpful in attracting more men to aerobic training programs.

5. _____ Cross-country skiing simulators provide a total body workout.

6. _____ The Versa climber simulates climbing a mountain.

7. _____ Strength training machines are relatively small pieces of equipment.

8. _____ Nautilus uses the compressed air resistance system.

9. _____ Much of the commercial equipment is available to the consumer.

10. _____ In regard to the machines that use the exerciser's own body weight to provide the resistance, the steeper the ramp, the greater the resistance.

III. Fill-In Questions

Read each statement carefully and fill in the space provided with the best response.

1. Explain why free weights have been incorporated into aerobic exercise routines._____

_____

2. List three pieces of aerobic exercise equipment. _____

_____

_____

3. What are the two most popular types of resistance systems?

_____

_____

ANSWERS FOR CHAPTER THREE

I. Multiple Choice Questions

1. c - p.257
2. b - p.258
3. d - p.258
4. a,d - p.258
5. b - p.259
6. a - p.259
7. c - p.261
8. d - p.261
9. a - p.261
10. b,d - p.262

II. True or False Items

1. False - p.257
2. True - p.258
3. True - p.259
4. True - p.260
5. True - p.261
6. False - p.261
7. False - p.261
8. False - p.262
9. True - p.263
10. True - p.264

III. Fill-In Questions

1. To increase the cardiovascular benefits while toning muscles. - p.257
2. Rowing machines; treadmills; rebounders. - p.258
3. Weight stacks and compressed air. - p.262

Appendix 1

Curriculum Objectives:
AFAA's National Primary Certification
For the Aerobic Exercise Professional

Purpose

The Aerobics and Fitness Association of America is an association of exercise professionals and enthusiasts, advised by a multidisciplinary Board of Advisors, dedicated to the goals of safety and excellence in fitness instruction. To meet these goals, in 1983, AFAA published the **Basic Exercise Standards and Guidelines**, establishing a standard of acceptable performance for aerobic exercise classes intended for the healthy adult population. In the same year, the AFAA Cetification for Aerobic Exercise Professionals was also created, thus providing the first nationwide standardized measure of instructor competency. In 1984, AFAA initiated its Instructor Training Program at authorized training centers.

Training is defined as the learning process through which one acquires the theory and practical skills necessary to teach exercise. Certification refers to the actual measurement, usually by examination, of the performance of practical skill and theoretical knowledge of exercise instructors. The following objectives were created to define fundamental theoretical knowledge and practical skills necessary for safe and effective exercise instruction, in preparation for Certification. These objectives apply to classes intended for average healthy adults without known physiological or biological conditions that would in any way restrict their exercise activities.

Part A: Professional Responsibility and Instructional Skills

The instructor should demonstrate knowledge of the principles involved in exercise program design and format, and the techniques for leading and monitoring an exercise class.

Safety

1. Discuss the role of the fitness instructor as it relates to exercise prescription and fitness testing. Cite AFAA's recommendations for stress testing prior to beginning an aerobic exercise program. List three methods for evaluating cardiovascular fitness, and one for evaluating musculoskeletal strength.
2. Discuss the importance of pre-exercise screening and medical clearance for high-risk individuals.
3. Demonstrate the ability to monitor pulse; explain procedures and precautions for radial and carotid sites. Discuss the length of time recommended for pulse-taking and frequency during class.
4. Define perceived exertion and explain its application to target heart rate range and its relationship to age and other variables.
5. Calculate target heart rate range through both Karvonnen and simplified methods.
6. Discuss methods of monitoring participants for signs of exercise intolerance, and list appropriate course of action.
7. Maintain current CPR card, and be familiar with on-site emergency protocols.
8. Demonstrate an ability to administer first aid for the following conditions: hyperventilation, choking, lightheadedness, chest pain, seizures, bleeding, fainting, nausea, acute muscular or skeletal pain, sprains, fractures, hives, allergic reaction, bronchospasm, hypoglycemic and diabetic reactions.
9. Describe heat exhaustion, heat cramps and heat stroke. List the symptoms, prevention and first aid.
10. Define R.I.C.E. and explain its appropriate use.
11. Explain the importance of a pre-exercise health screening form. List which congenital, genetic, or chronic physical conditions should be investigated. Explain the importance of inquiring about medications for heart, blood pressure, respiratory problems or other medical restrictions that might effect an individual's exercise performance.
12. Recognize conditions or problems that might require medical clearance prior to beginning a vigorous exercise program.

Pre-Class Procedure

1. Explain pre-class instructions that include: methods of monitoring pulse, target heart rate range, appropriate level of participation,

correct breathing, orientation to aerobics and proper attire and shoes.

2. Describe appropriate pre-class screening for participants, and discuss exercise guidelines for type of class, level of intensity, and modification of exercise based on an individual's age, fitness level and physical limitations.

3. Understand the effect of beta blocker medication on heart rate.

4. Discuss exercise precautions and modifications for individuals who are obese, or have musculoskeletal problems, such as weak back or knees.

5. Explain pre-class instructions for known or physical signs and symptoms of exercise intolerance, and appropriate course of action.

Practical Applications

1. Demonstrate anticipatory cueing techniques which lead students from one exercise to another with a smooth transition.

2. Demonstrate ability to recognize and correct poor alignment and incorrect execution of moves by students.

3. Demonstrate means for increasing or decreasing difficulty and/or complexity of movements. Explain progression of intensity during aerobic phase.

4. Demonstrate ability to coordinate appropriate music with respect to beats per minute to various phases of an exercise class.

5. Demonstrate leadership ability to guide individuals through non-competitive and appropriate levels of participation.

6. Demonstrate ways to modify movements to accommodate various fitness levels in one class.

7. Give recommendations for proper attire, use of nonpermeable clothing, appropriate aerobic shoes.

8. Explain adaptations for exercising in heat, cold and high humidity.

9. Explain an instructor's responsibility and liability in regard to participant's safety.

10. List and describe a safe and effective class sequence. Explain reasons for your selected sequence.

11. Outline how to adapt an exercise program to meet an individual's particular interests and goals, specifying exercises to develop cardiovascular endurance, exercises to develop muscular strength and muscular endurance, and exercises to improve flexibility and joint range of motion, utilizing the principles of intensity, duration, frequency, specificity and overload.

12. Understand the physiological process involved with warm-up activity by demonstrating a balanced combination of static stretches and rhythmic limbering exercises.

13. Discuss the differences between static stretch, rhythmic limbering exercises and ballistic movements in relation to the stretch reflex.
14. Demonstrate correct body alignment while performing static stretch, rhythmic limbering exercises, aerobics and muscular strengthening exercises in standing, sitting, and lying positions.
15. Demonstrate a smooth flow and sequence to warming-up the major muscle groups to be worked.
16. Explain the evaluation process in determining if an exercise is safe and effective. Cite examples and explain reasons for omitting certain exercises.

Part B: Basic Anatomy and Injury Prevention

The instructor should demonstrate knowledge in the area of basic anatomy and injury prevention as it applies to an exercise class.

Basic Anatomy

1. Describe the function and interrelationship of the heart, lungs, vascular system and respiratory system in the delivery of oxygen from the outside environment to the working tissues.
2. Identify the major muscle groups, their type and function.
3. Identify bones according to their shape classification.
4. Define muscle, bone, tendon, ligament, cartilage and nerve.
5. Identify the different types of joints, and explain their functions, citing examples.
6. Define and cite examples of the following anatomical descriptions: supine, prone, dorsal, plantar, anterior, posterior, lateral, medial, distal and proximal.
7. Discuss the effect of exercise on age-related bone development or deterioration.
8. Describe correct standing body alignment and posture.
9. Identify the five sections of the vertebral column and define lordosis, scoliosis and kyphosis.

Injury Prevention

1. Cite the AFAA guideline for instructors on recommended maximum number of classes taught per day and classes taught per week.
2. List and explain at least six symptoms of overtraining.
3. Discuss the most common precipitating factors responsible for back pain. Demonstrate correct postural alignment and modifications to exercises for protecting the low back.
4. Describe the following common injuries: shin splints, stress fractures, anterior compartment syndrome, chondromalacia patella,

plantar fasciitis, tendinitis, sprains, strains, bursitis, Morton's Syndrome, vocal chord strain and medial meniscus damage. Discuss techniques for prevention and resumption of activity post-injury.

5. Discuss the principle and importance of muscle balancing in regard to injury prevention, and cite examples.
6. Define R.I.C.E. Explain when to administer and when to seek medical help.
7. Explain the purpose of a post-aerobic cooldown, and its effect on cardiovascular and muscular systems. List methods for preventing muscle spasms, nausea, fainting and dizziness.
8. Identify and describe extrinsic factors that could prevent injuries: proper flooring, aerobic shoes, safety and environmental factors.
9. List the risk factors for cardiovascular disease. Identify which can be affected by lifestyle modifications and which cannot.
10. Discuss the ramifications of improper attire or fluid intake and its inhibition of the body's natural thermostatic controls.

Part C: Kinesiology and Biomechanics

The instructor should demonstrate knowledge of kinesiology and basic biomechanics in regard to body alignment and injury prevention.

1. Define and demonstrate proper body alignment in regard to center of gravity and skeletal balancing in the vertical plane.
2. Describe and demonstrate correct body alignment for both standing exercises and for floor exercises, such as side-lying.
3. Discuss and demonstrate techniques for reducing impact to the lower extremities which could cause joint stress.
4. List five exercise positions which cannot be performed without undue stress to joints or surrounding tissues.
5. Discuss how strengthening the abdominal muscles can help protect the lumbar spine. Describe the interrelationship between hip flexor and hamstring strength and flexibility in regard to low back protection.
6. Discuss flexibility exercises as a means of injury prevention.
7. Define agonist, antagonist, and synergist and their interrelationship.
8. Define flexion, extension, hyperflexion, and hyperextension. Demonstrate examples of each.
9. Define abduction, adduction, circumduction and rotation. Demonstrate examples of each.

10. Define supination, pronation, inversion and eversion, and demonstrate examples using the foot and ankle.
11. Identify the anatomical location and describe the major joint action of the following muscle groups. Demonstrate exercises that will stretch each muscle group. Demonstrate exercises that will strengthen each muscle group.
   a. Arms, chest, shoulder, upper and middle back:
      pectoralis major, deltoids, biceps, triceps, trapezius, rhomboids, latissimus dorsi
   b. Torso and lower back:
      rectus abdominis, internal/external obliques, erector spinae, quadratus lumborum
   c. Hips and buttocks:
      gluteus maximus, hip abductors, gluteus medius, tensor fascia latae
   d. Thighs and lower legs:
      quadricep femoris group, hamstring group, hip adductors, iliopsoas, gastrocnemius, tibialis anterior, soleus

Part D: Exercise Physiology

The instructor should demonstrate knowledge of the principles of exercise physiology as it applies to the exercise class setting.

Essentials of Basic Exercise Physiology

1. Identify the three major components of physical fitness.
2. Define specificity, overload, variability and reversability, and relate their importance in designing an exercise program.
3. Define and list training effects that will occur as a result of aerobic exercise.
4. Define and differentiate between aerobic and anaerobic activity. List examples of each.
5. Define frequency, intensity and duration. Explain the correlation between these principles in obtaining the benefits of aerobic exercise.
6. Compare and contrast the aerobic and anaerobic metabolic pathways in terms of fuel source, time, intensity, oxygen debt and breakdown of glucose.
7. Define aerobic capacity, steady state, anaerobic threshold and oxygen debt.
8. Explain the role of ATP as an energy source for aerobic and anaerobic exercise.

Cardiovascular Fitness

1. State a formula for determining target heart rate range.
2. Explain perceived exertion as a method of monitoring exercise response and appropriate times for its use.
3. List the benefits of aerobic exercise on the following: metabolism, stroke volume, cardiac output, oxygen uptake, resting pulse, blood pressure, respiratory changes, cellular changes, and body composition.
4. Describe the best means for maximizing the utilization of fat as a fuel for energy metabolism.
5. Describe the bell curve during the aerobic phase of an exercise class in terms of heart rate response and fitness level.
6. Discuss changes in fuel utilization and training effect when working below or above target heart rate range.
7. Discuss how to recognize when a training effect has occurred due to overload.

Flexibility

1. Discuss physiology of stretching: the stretch reflex, static vs. ballistic stretching, and techniques for increasing flexibility.
2. Discuss flexibility as a means of injury prevention and muscle balancing.
3. Discuss overflexibility and hyperextension in terms of joint instability.
4. Explain the difference between active versus passive stretching.
5. List specific stretching exercises that could cause joint stress.
6. Explain the difference in purpose between stretches performed during the warm-up and cool-down portions of an exercise class.
7. Explain the effects of a regular stretching protocol on improving joint range of motion and flexibility.
8. Demonstrate proper body alignment while stretching the major muscle groups of the body.
9. Explain the use of static stretch to dissipate lactic acid build up and alleviate muscle soreness.

Muscular Endurance and Strength

1. Define and compare muscular strength and muscular endurance.
2. Discuss strength development as related to specificity of training and overload.
3. Define muscle hypertrophy and atrophy.
4. Explain how to recognize the results of training effect.

5. Define the following: periodization, progression, overload, muscle fatigue and muscle failure.
6. Describe the following types of contractions: isometric, isotonic, isokinetic, concentric and eccentric.
7. Explain the importance of rest as part of a muscular strengthening program to physiologically allow the body to recover and rebuild.
8. Explain the difference in training techniques, in relationship to repetitions, sets and weights, when building for "bulk" versus building for "tone."
9. Explain the danger and consequences of breath holding when performing isometric exercises.
10. Demonstrate strengthening exercises for major muscle groups using proper body alignment and posture.
11. Discuss the difference between muscular work and muscular movement in relationship to speed, isolation, momentum and resistance.

Part E: Sports Nutrition and Body Composition

The instructor should demonstrate a knowledge of sports nutrition and body composition.

1. Identify the seven nutrients essential for life and discuss the basic principle of dietary balance for optimum health.
2. Discuss fluids and the regulation of body temperature during exercise. Cite the best sources for re-hydration. Discuss the use of electrolyte drinks by endurance athletes.
3. Compare calories per gram of carbohydrates, fats and proteins, and current American Heart Association recommended percentages of each group for a balanced daily diet.
4. Discuss the risks involved with taking megadoses of vitamins and/or minerals.
5. Explain the principles of energy balance relating to caloric intake and exercise output.
6. State recommended maximum weight loss in terms of number of pounds per week, when not under a physician's care.
7. Explain the benefits of a high carbohydrate, low fat diet as it relates to exercise.
8. Define carbohydrate loading and cite precautions for its use.
9. Understand special recommendations for nutrient supplementation for vegetarians, females, athletes and pregnant women.
10. Discuss fallacies in regard to spot reduction, "sweating off pounds of fat," cellulite and herbal wraps.

11. Discuss the principles of overfat versus overweight.
12. Discuss ratio of lean body mass to body fat and total body weight, listing ideal ranges for body fat percentages for men and women.
13. List four ways of measuring percent body fat. Discuss drawbacks in using traditional height/weight charts.
14. Discuss osteoporosis and its relation to exercise, aging, estrogen and calcium supplements.
15. Discuss the effects of a regular aerobic exercise regime on HDL, LDL and serum cholesterol ratios.
16. Explain precautions in regard to the use of salt tablets, liquid diets, high-protein diets, starvation diets, diuretics and diet pills.
17. Define and describe the symptoms of nutritional disorders, including anorexia nervosa, bulimia, hypoglycemia and diabetes.
18. Identify the symptoms of a food allergic reaction.
19. Know how to calculate an individual's Basal Metabolic Rate (BMR) and determine the individual's recommended daily caloric intake in order to lose weight, gain weight or maintain weight.

The AFAA International Primary Certification Examination Criteria

I. Examination Objective

A. The written examination is intended to test the participant's understanding of the theoretical aspects of aerobic exercise and the ability to educate and motivate others in the areas of health and fitness. AFAA's Primary Written Examination covers areas dealing with the healthy adult only. Specialty areas such as the physically challenged, the overweight, pre- and post-natal, seniors, low-impact and the use of low weights will be assessed separately.

II. Format and Scoring

A. The written examination consists of one hundred multiple choice, true/false and matching type questions. Examinees will have one hour to complete the exam. The successful candidate must correctly answer 80% of the questions.

B. The AFAA Primary Written Examination is overseen by the National Fitness Testing Council (NFTC), an educational testing board that verifies and insures the validity and format of the Certification Examination.

III. Content and Preparation

A. Listed below are the subject areas covered on the Primary Written Exam and the corresponding chapters for study in **Aerobics: Theory and Practice**, Aerobics and Fitness Association of America, 1985.

Subject	Chapter
Class Conduct	Basic Exercise Standards and Guidelines xiii
	Part A—Chapters 4,7
	Part B—Chapter 2, Appendix A
Sports Physiology	Part A—Chapters 1,2,4,7,9
Body Composition	Part A—Chapter 5
Anatomy	Part A—Chapter 2
Injury Prevention	Part A—Chapters 13,14
Cardiovascular/Medical Considerations	Part A—Chapters 2,3,4,7
	Part B—Chapter 1
	Appendix C
Basic Nutrition	Part A—Chapter 6,8
Exercise Technique	Basic Exercise Standards and Guidelines xiii
	Part A—Chapter 10
	Part B—Chapter 2
	Appendix B
Sports Psychology	Part A—Chapter 12
	Part B—Chapter 4

The AFAA International Primary Certification Practical Examination Component

I. Criteria

A. Eligibility

Candidates attempting the practical exam should be experienced aerobic exercise instructors. Health status should in no way infringe on their ability to correctly demonstrate required exercises.

B. Standard of Correct Performance

All eligible examinees shall be judged on their ability to correctly demonstrate aerobics and strengthening exercise for the major muscle groups. The Standards by which examinees shall be judged are those outlined in the "Basic Exercise Standards and Guidelines of the Aerobics and Fitness Association of America." Correct performance shall be generally defined as demonstrating the required exercises in such a way as to provide training potential, without known physiological risk to the average class participant.

C. Categories of Examination

Candidates shall be examined in the following categories:

1. Warm-up: Rhythmic limbering exercise/static stretch
2. Aerobics
3. Rhythm and Coordination
4. Arms/Chest/Shoulders/Back
5. Quadriceps/Hip Flexors
6. Buttocks/Hamstrings
7. Hip Abduction
8. Abdominal exercise

    9. Hip Adduction
10. Cooldown
11. Posture
12. Instructional Technique
13. Presentation
14. Overall Assessment

II.   Evaluation

A. Examiners

Candidates shall be evaluated by a panel of three examiners, all of whom have completed training in the examination process.

B. Scoring

Candidates shall be evaluated in each category by all three examiners. The high score and the low score will be discarded, leaving the middle score (mode) as the final score in each category.

Scores range from 1-5 as follows:

1. Unacceptable
2. Unsatisfactory
3. Satisfactory
4. Good
5. Excellent

C. Passing Score

A passing score for the Practical Exam is 42. This represents achieving a score of 3 in each of the 14 categories.

D. Test Results

Examination results shall be mailed to each examinee, regardless of whether or not a passing score is achieved. Deficiencies and unsatisfactory performance areas shall be noted.

No telephone inquiries.

E. Re-Testing

Examinees not achieving a passing score are encouraged to re-test. Re-testing may occur at any regularly scheduled Primary Certification Workshop. Examinees should not attempt to be re-tested until such time as they have identified and corrected the unsatisfactory areas of performance as noted on their examination results. Re-testing must be scheduled in advance through the AFAA International Headquarters located in California.

III.   Testing Description

A. Duration

The exam is approximately one hour and twenty minutes in duration. No observers shall be allowed in the testing areas. Late arrivals shall not be admitted once the exam has begun.

B. Attire

Examinees should wear tights and leotards, or shorts and T-shirts. No sweat pants or other bulky or restrictive pants or shirts will be permitted. Athletic shoes must be worn. Black soled shoes are not allowed. Assigned testing number should be pinned on the chest. Exercise mats may be used.

C. Practical Examination Format, Part I

Candidates shall be evaluated in groups of approximately 20 persons. The Lead examiner shall announce the category to be demonstrated. All examinees will then simultaneously demonstrate exercises appropriate for that category. Exercises are demonstrated without verbal explanation. Examinees should continue demonstrating exercises for that category until requested to change category. Time allotments will vary. The order and minimum requirements of Part I are listed below:

1. Warm-up. Examinee must demonstrate in any order, a minimum of 2 static stretches EACH for the upper body, middle body and the lower body, and a minimum of 3 rhythmic limbering exercises.
2. Aerobics. Examinees will have approximately 4-5 minutes to demonstrate:
   a. gradual increase of intensity
   b. building a sequence or combination
   c. variety of movement patterns
   d. gradual decrease of intensity (a cue will be provided)
3. Arms/chests/shoulders/back. Examinees must demonstrate with resistance a minimum of 4 exercises.
4. Quadriceps/hip flexor exercises. Examinees must demonstrate a minimum of 3 exercises.
5. Abdominal exercises. Examinees must demonstrate a minimum of 4 exercises as follows:
   a. 1 exercise isolating the rectus abdominis as the primary mover.
   b. 1 exercise, minimum, isolating the obliques.

        c. 1 exercise, minimum, demonstrated with the feet
elevated.

6. Hip abduction. Examinees must demonstrate a minimum
of 3 exercises.
7. Buttocks/hamstrings. Examinees must demonstrate a
minimum of 3 exercises in two or more postures.
8. Hip adduction. Examinees must demonstrate a minimum
of 3 exercises.
9. Cooldown. Examinees must demonstrate a minimum of
2 upper body and 2 lower body static stretches.

D. Format, Part II

During approximately the last 20 minutes of the exam, candidates shall be called forward individually to teach the other
examinees. The examinee shall have approximately 1 minute
to instruct the other examinees in at least one exercise from
an exercise category announced by the Lead Examiner. This
portion of the exam will include verbal presentation. Examiners will evaluate examinees on Instructional Technique and
Presentation.

E. Music

Music with a standard 4/4 beat shall be supplied. This will
be the same music that is used throughout the workshops.

IV. Preparation

A. AFAA Primary Certification Workshops

Instructors desiring an in-depth review should attend the
2-day Primary Certification Workshop. Examinations are
administered at conclusion of Workshop.

B. AFAA Certification Review

Skilled instructors requiring a brief review should attend an
AFAA Certification Review offered exclusively by AFAA Certification Specialists. Exams are administered at the conclusion of the Review. Reviews are held 20-30 times per month.

C. AFAA Training

Both 20-hour and 40-hour instructor training curriculums are
available from authorized AFAA Trainers. These intensive and
comprehensive courses are appropriate for the novice or the
instructor who desires a formal training program. Upon
completion, individuals are prepared to take the Certification
Exams.

D. Recommended Reading

See Appendix 4.

E. Instructional Video

© 1986 Copyright Aerobics and Fitness Association of America, revised, 1986. This material may not be utilized or reproduced in whole or in part for any purpose without the express written consent of the Aerobics and Fitness Association of America in each instance.

Suggested Reading List

A erobics and Fitness Association of America, **Aerobics: Theory and Practice** (Costa Mesa, CA: HDL Publ., 1985)

For a more in-depth study, beyond what is required for the AFAA Primary level Certification Examination, please refer to the following suggested reading list:

Instructional Practice

Aerobics and Fitness Association of America. **Aerobics: Theory and Practice** (Costa Mesa, CA: HDL Publ., 1985)

Alter, J., **Surviving Exercise** (Boston: Houghton Mifflin, 1983).

Hockey, R., **Physical Fitness** (St. Louis: Mosby, 1981).

Pollock, M. and Wilmore, J., **Health and Fitness Through Physical Activity** (New York: Wiley, 1978).

Basic Anatomy and Injury Prevention

American College of Sports Medicine, **Guidelines for Graded Exercise Testing and Exercise Prescription, 2nd Ed.** (Philadelphia: Lea and Febiger, 1986).

Cooper, K.H. **The Aerobics Program for Total Well Being** (New York: M. Evans, 1982).

Donnely, J., **Living Anatomy** (Champaign, IL: Human Kinetics Publishers, 1984).

Fox, E. and Mathews, D., **The Physiological Basis of Physical Education and Athletics** (New York: Saunders College Publishing, 1981).

Herbert, D.L. and Herbert, W.G., **Legal Aspects of Preventive and Rehabilitative Exercise Programs** (Canton, OH: Professional and Executive Reports, 1984).

Landley, L. and Telford, I., **Dynamic Anatomy and Physiology, 5th Ed.** (Champaign, IL: Human Kinetics Publishers, 1980).

Patton, B., McCorrey, J., and Gettman, L., **Implementing Health and Fitness Programs** (Champaign, IL: Human Kinetics Publishers, 1976).

Sharkey, B., **Principles of Human Anatomy** (New York: Harper & Row, 1980).

Exercise Physiology

American College of Sports Medicine, "The Recommended Quantity and Quality of Exercise for Developing and Maintaining Fitness in Healthy Adults." (Position Statement.) 1978.

Clarke, D. "Adaptations in Strength and Muscular Endurance Resulting from Exercise." Exercise and Sports Sciences Review. New York: Academic Press, 1973.

deVries, H., **Physiology of Exercise for Physical Education and Athletics, 2nd Ed.** (Dubuque, IA.)

Getchell, B., **Physical Fitness: A Way of Life** (New York: Wiley, 1983).

Sharkey, B., **Physiology of Fitness, 3rd Ed.** (Champaign, IL: Human Kinetics Publishers, 1984).

Wenger, N., Ed., **Exercise and the Heart** (Philadelphia: Davis, 1985).

Wilmore, J., **Training for Sport and Activity, 2nd Ed.** (Boston: Allyn and Bacon, 1982).

Kinesiology and Biomechanics

Rasch, R., and Burke, P., **Kinesiology and Applied Anatomy, 6th Ed.** (Philadelphia: Lea and Febiger, 1978).

Strauss, R., Ed., **Sports Medicine** (Philadelphia: Saunders, 1984).

Wells, K. and Luttgens, K., **Kinesiology: Scientific Basis of Human Motion** (Philadelphia: W. B. Saunders, 1982).

Sports Nutrition and Body Composition

Bailey, C., **Fit or Fat** (Boston: Houghton Mifflin, 1977).

Coleman, E., **Eating For Endurance** (Riverside, CA: Rubidoux Printing Co., 1980).

Katch, F. and McArdle, W., **Nutrition, Weight Control and Exercise, 2nd Ed.** (Philadelphia: Lea and Febiger, 1984).

Lohmon, T. "Body Composition Methodology in Sports Medicine." **Physician and Sportsmedicine** 1982:10- (December: 47-58).

McArdle, W. et al. **Exercise Physiology—Energy, Nutrition and Human Performance, 2nd Ed.** (Philadelphia: Lea and Febiger, 1986).

National Academy of Sciences, **Recommended Dietary Allowances, 9th Ed.** (Washington, DC: 1980).

The Nutritional Foundation, Inc., **Present Knowledge in Nutrition, 5th Ed.** (Washington, DC: 1984).

Pollack, M. et al. **Exercise in Health and Disease—Evaluation and Prescription for Prevention and Rehabilitation** (Philadelphia: Saunders Co., 1984).

William, S., **Essentials of Nutrition and Diet Therapy, 3rd Ed.** (St. Louis: Mosby, 1982).

Basic Exercise Standards and Guidelines
of the
Aerobics and Fitness Association of America™

These Standards represent an ongoing process of research, critique and consensus by a multidisciplinary team of aerobic industry leaders. Introduced in 1983, AFAA's Standards and Guidelines were the first nationally developed tools used by instructors. This revised 1987 edition reflects a higher level of sophistication and accuracy achieved by applying the most up-to-date research findings to the practice of aerobics.

I. Basic Principles, Definitions and Recommendations

All standards and guidelines outlined as follows apply to an average adult without known physiological or biological conditions that would in any way restrict their exercise activities.

A. Components of Physical Fitness

A complete physical fitness program should seek to improve and maintain:
1. Cardiovascular efficiency and endurance
2. Muscular strength and endurance
3. Flexibility
4. Optimal Body Composition

B. Principles of Training

1. Training Effect

Improvement, or creating a TRAINING EFFECT, refers to the physiological changes that occur in the body as a result of exercise. A training effect will only occur if the exercise is sufficient in all of the following areas.

a. duration: length of time
b. intensity: degree of strength, energy, or difficulty
c. frequency: how often performed

2. Overload Principle

Training occurs when the body is regularly stimulated (frequency), by periodically increasing INTENSITY, FREQUENCY and/or DURATION of exercise. The body responds by increasing its capacity to perform work and adapt to increasing physiological demands. This principal applies to all types of physical conditioning.

3. Application

An effective fitness program seeks to exercise the body beyond its normal workloads (overload), utilizing the training principles of FREQUENCY, INTENSITY, and DURATION to create a TRAINING EFFECT. A TRAINING EFFECT will occur when muscles are worked slightly beyond their point of fatigue, on a regular basis with increased FREQUENCY, INTENSITY, and DURATION. It is not necessary to "go for the burn" in order to create a "burn," which makes continued muscular contraction impossible and may hinder improvements in muscular endurance training.

4. Specificity of Training

Specificity refers to training specifically for an activity or isolating the specific muscle groups that one would like to improve. For example, a marathon runner will train for the event by running distance not wind sprints, because the marathon is an endurance activity.

C. Frequency of Training

1. Maintaining fitness is accomplished by a minimum of 3 workouts evenly spaced throughout the week. Detraining occurs within 2 1/2 weeks following cessation of exercise.

2. Improving fitness is achieved by participating in a minimum of 4-5 workouts per week. Individuals beginning an exercise program should begin with 3 workouts per week or as indicated by qualified exercise prescription. Additional workouts should be added only after an individual has become accustomed to the present level of exercise.

3. Overtraining

The body needs time to rest, recover, and rebuild from the stress of vigorous exercise. Instructors and students should be aware of the following symptoms of overtraining:

- fatigue

- anemia
- amenorrhea
- stress-related injuries
  a. stress fractures
  b. tendinitis
  c. bursitis
  d. shin splints
4. Teaching Fitness
As an instructor, be aware of the symptoms of overtraining as outlined above. Individual differences in the number of classes per week that an instructor can teach without risk of overtraining depend on the following variables:
a. level of fitness
b. length of time (experience) instructing any one particular type of fitness class
c. type of class one is teaching
d. degree of active demonstration
e. other fitness activities outside of teaching
Twelve classes per week including no more than 2 high impact classes per day should be the maximum for the experienced instructor.

D. Muscle Balancing
1. Principle
For every primary muscle worked (agonist), the opposing muscle group (antagonist) should also be worked. Example: biceps/triceps. By exercising opposing muscle groups, one lessens the possibility of muscular imbalance, thus reducing the potential for injury. Repeating the same exercises month after month works the muscles only through that range of motion, likewise stressing the joint and its attachments in the same areas over and over. A variety of exercises that strengthen both agonist and antagonist muscle groups will balance and improve joint stability.
2. Muscle Balancing and Posture
Many postural problems, Low Back Syndrome being the most common, are due to muscular imbalances. These imbalances are manifested by:
a.increased lumbar curve
b.shortened and contracted illiopsoas

    c.shortened and contracted hamstrings
    d.weak abdominals
    e.hyperextended knees
    f. rounded upper back and forward shoulders
    g.supinated or pronated feet

3. Application
Muscular imbalance causes the stronger muscle groups to compensate for the work of the weaker muscles. Injury occurs most often when both the applied stresses to and the support of the skeletal system are unequally distributed among the muscles.

To achieve a balanced posture and avoid the risk of Low Back Syndrome:
a. strengthen abdominals and quadriceps
b. increase flexibility of back and hamstrings
c. lengthen and release iliopsoas with pelvic tilts
d. stand and exercise maintaining proper body alignment (see following section)
e. perform exercises regularly for optimum strengthening/lengthening training effect
f. include exercises that concentrate on balance, muscle isolation, posture and body awareness
g. avoid hyperextension of the knee while standing because this tilts the pelvis forward, causing the lower back to arch and places excessive stress on the lumbar spine
h. avoid arching or back bends as these compress the lumbar spine, possibly resulting in pain and/or damage to the vertebral discs.

E. Body Alignment
When performing any exercises, be conscious of body alignment and posture. Stand tall, yet keep posture relaxed, not tense. Imagine a "midline" running from the top of the head down through the middle of the body. Keep body weight balanced and evenly distributed in relation to this imaginary midline. Abdominal muscles should be held firmly in with rib cage lifted and shoulders back and relaxed. Do not hyperextend (lock) knee or elbow joints. Hyperextension places excess stress on ligaments and tendons that attach at each joint, increasing potential for injury as well as decreasing the effectiveness of stretching or strengthening activities.

F. Speed, Isolation and Resistance

Exercises should be performed at a moderate speed that will allow full range of motion and concentrated work within the isolated muscles which are the focus of the exercise. Isolation of a muscle requires that an exercise be specific to the joint action (ex, flexion, extension, abduction). This isolation causes the muscle to contract and perform beyond the point of fatigue. Also isolation may cause other muscle groups to compensate by taking over in order to continue work.

Performing an exercise too quickly will often make this desired type of controlled movement impossible and lead to joint or muscle injury. Strengthening a muscle requires working the muscle against resistance in a controlled, deliberate manner. Resistance is supplied in one of two ways:

1. Through the use of external weights. (See AFAA's Weighted Workout Guidelines, c 1986, revised 1988).
2. By concentrating the tension of muscular contraction working against gravity.

Exercises performed too quickly often rely on momentum instead of actual muscle work. Slow, controlled resistive movements demand more muscular work than those movements which are fast and ballistic in nature.

G. Full Range of Motion

1. Normal Range of Motion

The full degree of movement that a lever is capable of as restricted by the joint and surrounding tissues. Full range of motion is desirable because (1), it will elicit a response from the greatest number of muscle fibers and, (2) it maintains adequate joint-mobility.

2. Application

The working muscle(s) should extend through the full range of motion dictated by the flexibility of the muscles and joints involved. Proper form and body alignment should be maintained and hypertension should be avoided. To work the muscles efficiently, move through the full range of motion required to complete each exercise.

II. Class Format

A. Sequence

This is a guideline to class design and format that is physiologically sound and effective and can be appropriately adapted to fit most club policies or your personal preference. Only in certain types of exercise categories such as warm-up or cool-down, are the specific exercise types important. The following is a recommended sequence used by AFAA for a one hour class:

1. Pre-class instruction.
2. Warm-up: A balanced combination of static stretching and rhythmic limbering exercises.
3. Exercises from the following groups, performed in a standing position, in order of preference:
   a. Aerobics and post-aerobic cool-down
   b. Arms, chest, shoulders and back strengthening
   c. Waist work
   d. Standing leg work
4. Dropping to the floor for the remainder of the class, exercises from the following groups may be performed in order of preference:
   a. Legs
   b. Buttocks
   c. Hips
   d. Abdominals
5. Cool-down: static stretching

B. Purpose of Sequence

The above sequence is effective because it will help to keep the flow of the class smooth. Getting up and down off the floor repeatedly creates "exercise gaps" and can cause rise and fall of heart rate within the aerobic segment. Strive for smooth transitions between exercise activities. Repeatedly stopping class is not only choppy and inconsistent but a sure way to lose the interest of the class. Keeping the class moving will maintain the energy and interest level.

The following recommendations should be adhered to regardless of class format used:

1. **Always begin class with warm-ups.**
2. **Always end class with static stretching.**
3. **Always follow aerobics with a sufficient cool-down period, including hamstring and calf stretches.**

4. Upon completion of strengthening exercises **within a specific muscle group, always stretch those muscles before proceeding to the next group.**
5. **During aerobic portion, movement should be continuous without abrupt stopping and starting or peak high and low activity.**

C. Class Level

Unless class level is specific, i.e., beginner or advanced, it is best to teach at an intermediate level and explain to the class how to adjust the individual exercises to their particular level of fitness and experience. In other words, try to give both a beginning and advanced version of your exercises while performing at an intermediate level. Motor skill, intensity, and duration capability of individuals must be considered.

III. Instructional Methods, Concerns and Responsibility

A. Monitoring - Purpose
1. Maximizing exercise effectiveness
2. Injury prevention
   a. Monitoring your students for alignment or performance errors is important in preventing musculoskeletal injury.
   b. Know the following danger signs. Should you observe any one of these or should a class participant complain of any of these, he/she should stop vigorous exercise immediately. If necessary, refer to on-site emergency procedures.
   • unusual fatigue
   • nausea
   • dizziness
   • tightness or pain in chest
   • lightheadedness
   • loss of muscle control
   • severe breathlessness
   • allergic reactions, i.e., rash/hives
   • blurring of vision
   Individual should contact his/her physician or obtain immediate medical advice. Always maintain your CPR certification at an up-to-date status.

B. Cueing

It is essential that vocal commands are used while instructing. A routine seems to flow more smoothly when the class is cued as to what the next exercise will be. ANTICIPATÓRY CUES are key words and small phrases which describe an exercise or a sequence which will be performed next.

It is also important when teaching exercise, that you strongly concentrate on body alignment. An exercise that is done incorrectly may not only be unsafe, but may lack any real benefit. It is essential that you as an instructor give BODY ALIGNMENT CUES for every exercise and make the necessary verbal corrections during the class.

C. Legal Responsibilities

1. To successfully defend against exercise injury lawsuits, instructors should complete training and certification programs that test both theoretical knowledge and performance skills, should practice according to a nationally accepted standard, and should carry a personal liability insurance.

2. It is advisable for instructors and club owners to consult an attorney to prepare a disclaimer and release that is in accordance with state and local laws in which the exercise club exists.

3. In addition, clubs should seek program review and approval by a medical advisory board.

IV.   Pre-Class Procedure

A. Medical Clearance

1. Physical Exam

Before class, determine if there are any new class members and the level of their experience. AFAA recommends a medical physical examination for all students who have not been exercising regularly, unless they are under 30 years of age and have had a satisfactory check-up within the past year. If between ages 30 and 34, the check-up should have been within the last three months and should include a resting EKG. For participants ages 35 and over, a medical examination and testing should include a stress EKG where the pulse reaches the level it would during aerobic workouts. Anyone with a pre-

existing medical condition should be screened by his or
her physician prior to beginning an exercise program.
2. Risk Factors
Some medical limitations and lifestyle habits require
modified programs and specific recommendations. An individual who demonstrates or acknowledges one or more
of the following should be advised to have a physical exam and exercise stress test prior to beginning an exercise
program.
a. increased resting heart rate
b. increased blood pressure
c. history of heart disease, either personally or genetically
d. cigarette smoking
e. high cholesterol
f. high triglycerides
g. poor eating habits
h. sedentary lifestyle
When one or more risk factors are present, extra precautions must be taken prior to exercising as some activities
may be contraindicated.
3. Effects of Drugs and/or Medication
Certain medications such as antihistamines and an-
tibiotics will elicit side effects during exercise similar to
the danger signs listed above. Some medications can alter
heart rates. For example, beta blockers suppress heart
rate activity. It is not recommended that individuals
engage in vigorous activity when taking drugs or medication. Individuals desiring to continue their exercise
regimen should be advised to consult their physician
regarding possible side effects.

B. Introductions
Introduce yourself and announce the level of the class.

C. Attire
If some class members are without shoes, AFAA strongly
recommends they obtain and use shoes designed for aerobic
exercise as a means of reducing the risk of injury to feet,
knees and shins. This should be explained to the class, and
the criteria for appropriate shoes discussed.

D. Level of Participation
Explain that the class is non-competitive and that all participants should work at their own level. Make sure the class

is aware of danger signs as outlined in III, A. above. In case of any sharp pain experienced while exercising, the activity should be discontinued immediately and be discussed with the instructor following class.

E. Breathing
Breathing should follow a consistent rhythmic pattern throughout the class. The level of activity will reflexly dictate rate and depth of ventilation. Do not restrict inhalation to the nose. Inspire and expire through the nose and mouth in a relaxed fashion. Holding your breath while exercising may induce Valsalva manuever, closing the glottis and creating an unequal pressure in the chest cavity which may cause a rise in blood pressure. By the same token, hyperventilating or breathing too hard while exercising can irritate the nasal passage as well as cause lightheadedness.

F. Orientation to Aerobics
Define aerobics for new members. Explain before class how they can find their own target zone for aerobic work and how and where to take a pulse count.

V.   "Warm-Up"

A. Purpose
Prepares the body for vigorous exercises and reduces the risk of injury.

B. Time
Class should begin with 8-12 minutes of a balanced combination of static stretches and smoothly performed, rhythmic limbering exercises.

C. Stretching
Correctly performed stretching will increase the capacity for full range of movement. This allows one to perform more smoothly with less risk of injury.
  1. Muscle length
      a. Resting length—length of a muscle at rest
      b. Maximum length—the degree to which a muscle length can be stretched at any particular time.
      c. Increasing length—repeated stretching of a muscle over a period of time will gradually increase the resting length of the muscle fibers.

2. Static stretch

   Stretches performed in a group exercise setting should be static, non-ballistic. Static stretches are sustained stretches in a supportive position which allows the muscle being stretched to relax and elongate. Ballistic movement is forcefully executed and cannot be accomplished with the muscle relaxed. Ballistic movement, such as bouncing during a stretch, invokes the stretch reflex. Stretching is most effective if it is done slowly and gently without bouncing.

3. Stretch reflex

   The stretch reflex is the body's automatic protective mechanism against severe injury and abuse. Whenever a muscle is stretched quickly and with force or beyond the limits of the body's flexibility, a reflex is initiated which causes the muscle being stretched to contract to protect and prevent injury and overstretching.

4. Position

   Always assume a position with the body correctly aligned and supported so that the stretch will occur along the muscle's longitudinal line. Example: in a calf stretch, do not turn the back foot out. Both feet should face the same direction so hips are square to the front leg and a calf stretch can be performed.

5. How to Stretch

   Begin slowly in an easy stretch and not to maximum muscle length. Stretch to the point of mild tension and hold. As the tension relaxes, increase stretch slightly until point of tension is reached. If tension is painful, ease off slightly. Breathing should be slow, rhythmic and controlled. Length of time that a stretch is held will vary according to whether or not one is stretching at the beginning of class when muscles are cold, or at the end of class when muscles are warm.

D. Sequence

In order to maintain a smooth flow to your warm-up, one should follow a specific order that will include all major muscle groups. Warm-up from either the head to the toes, or vice-versa, i.e., don't skip from the neck to the ankles to the arms to the calves.

E. Muscle Groups

AFAA recommends that all of the following muscle groupings be warmed-up at the beginning of class:

1. Head and neck (sternocleidomastoid, levator scapula, trapezius (occipital portion).
2. Upper back, middle back, shoulders (trapezius, rhomboids, latissimus dorsi, teres major and minor, serratus anterior, and the anterior, medial and posterior deltoid).
3. Chest and arms (pectoralis major and minor, biceps, triceps, brachioradialis, brachialis).
4. Rib cage, waist and lower back (rectus abdominis, external and internal obliques, erector spinae, quadratus lumborum).
5. Front and back of thighs (quadricep femoris group, hamstring group, sartorius).
6. Outer thigh and upper hip (tensor fascia latae, gluteus medius).
7. Inner thigh (adductors longus, brevis magnus, pectineus, gracilis).
8. Calf and front of shin (gastrocnemius, soleus, tibialis anterior).
9. Feet and ankles (flexors and extensors).

F. Rhythmic Limbering Exercises

These exercises, performed at a smooth and moderate pace, help prepare your body for more vigorous exercise by increasing flexibility of the joint and its attachments, raising muscle temperature, increasing circulation to the tissues surrounding the joints, and maximizing neuromuscular function.

Examples: arm circles, lunges side to side, small kicks, knee lifts, alternating arm reaches.

G. Special Do's and Don'ts

1. Do warm up and stretch the lower back before attempting any lateral movement of the upper torso, i.e., side bends.
2. Don't do traditional toe touches to stretch the hamstrings. Roll down with knees bent, partially straighten one leg, keeping hips square and hold, relax. Alternate legs. Come up from this position by uncurling with knees bent.

3. Don't do full deep knee bends (grand plies), as this strains the cruciate ligaments in the knee.
4. Don't do "the plow," as this position could cause injury to the neck. The vertebrae and discs in the cervical area were not designed to withstand this type of pressure.
5. Don't do the "hurdler's stretch" as it places extreme tension on the medial ligaments of the knee.

H. Special Considerations
1. Spinal flexion—forward
   Although the spine was meant to flex forward, hanging with the torso in an unsupported position with gravity pulling downward on the back can place stress on the vertebrae in the lumbar region as well as increase the potential for overstretching muscles and ligaments in the spine. Ligaments have little elasticity. Once over-stretched they remain elongated, decreasing the support they offer in the lower back.

   Follow these guidelines for performing exercises which require spinal flexion:
   a. When stretching, or performing limbering rhythmic movements, all movements should be performed in a con-trolled manner.
   b. Do not maintain any forward flexed position for an ex-tended period of time, as overstretching of the ligaments in the lower back may occur.
   c. Always support the torso by flexing from the hip joint, placing hands on the lower portion of the thigh above the knee. Avoid arching backwards. Never let arms just hang down.
   d. Hold abdominals up and in to protect the lower back. By holding the abdominals in and up, the internal organs are supported by the abdominal muscles, instead of pull-ing down on the lower back.
   e. Keep hips above knee level. Allowing the hips to drop below the knees places stress on the ligament in the knees as well as the back.
   f. Always roll up from a bent over position, with the knees relaxed.
   g. When stretching hamstrings from a standing or seated position, lead with chest and bend from the hips.

Do not bend from the waist or back, arching the back and dropping the head. Head should always be in alignment with the spine.

2. Lateral spinal flexion
Stretching to the side unsupported for a long period of time can be just as stressful as anterior spinal flexion IF performed incorrectly. When performing any type of lateral stretch, support the torso with one hand on waist or thigh with hips squared. Never lean so far over to the side that you are "hanging" and have to throw one hip out of alignment to support the back. Nor should lateral flexion be performed with both arms extended over the head. These positions can be potentially dangerous and can cause ligamental damage. Individuals who can stretch sideways to a horizontal position are usually relying on ligaments that have been overstretched in past activities, by forcing or bouncing to increase flexibility.

VI. Upper Body

A. Purpose
To strengthen and improve muscular endurance of the arms, chest, shoulders and back.

B. Time
5-7 minutes

C. Arms, Chest, Shoulders and Back
Exercises may be performed with the lower body in a stationary position, with limited movement, or they may be incorporated with the aerobics. If performed during the aerobics, keep footwork simple so that the upper body muscle groups may be the area of concentrated work. Always include exercises that will work the opposing muscle groups for muscle balancing.

D. Method
Please refer to Section I, F, 1 and 2.

E. Position

In a standing, stationary position, maintain correct body alignment. Abdominals should be held in firmly, rib cage lifted, knees relaxed with buttocks tucked. The same upper body alignment should be applied when performing arm work during aerobics. Do not use momentum to pull shoulders backward or round shoulders forward as this can cause unnecessary strain on the back.

F. Push-ups

Push-ups performed with either straight legs or on the knees, can be an excellent exercise for strengthening the muscles of the arms and chest. In order to perform push-ups safely, the following should be noted:

1. In order to protect the lower back, it is advisable to slightly raise the buttocks.
2. Elbows should not lock or overbend.
3. Head should be held straight in a natural extension of the spine.

VII.   Aerobics

A. Aerobics

A variety of exercises which creates an increased demand for oxygen over an extended period of time. Aerobic exercises train the cardiovascular system to process and deliver oxygen quickly and efficiently to every part of the body. As the heart muscle becomes stronger and more efficient, a larger volume of blood is able to be pumped with each stroke and with fewer strokes, thus facilitating the rapid transport of oxygen to all parts of the body with less stress on the heart. An aerobically fit cardiovascular system will allow the individual to work longer, more vigorously and to recover more quickly.

B. Time

20-30 minutes

C. Sequence

The aerobic portion should resemble a normal bell curve. Start slowly and gradually increase the intensity and range of motion of our aerobic movements. Avoid lateral high impact moves during the first three minutes to allow your ankles and feet to become sufficiently warmed up. Peak movements, that is large movements using both arms and legs requiring a greater amount of oxygen to be delivered to the muscles, should be interspersed with lower intensity aerobic patterns to maintain steady state. These peak movements should not be included during the first three minutes.

D. Position

Correct posture (refer to Section I, E) with the abdominals held firmly in should be maintained throughout aerobics. Heels should always come all the way down to the floor. Don't jog on your toes, as this shortens the calf muscles and Achilles tendon. Do not lean forward, as this can contribute to shin splints. Do keep body weight balanced forward over entire foot and not backwards on heels.

E. Type of Movements

Try to vary your movements in order to both maintain interest level and effectively work as many muscles as possible. Combination moves requiring coordination of both arms and legs should be entered into slowly, starting with either the arms or the legs and then adding the other. Build upon your moves instead of trying to teach a complicated combination movement all at once. Choose moves that are appropriate for the fitness level of the class. Avoid extended periods of jumping or high leg kicks. Do not jump on just one leg for more than 8 times in succession because of risk of injury caused by repeated impact.

F. Breathing

Steady, rhythmic breathing, through both the nose and mouth should be used. Breath holding should be avoided in aerobic rhythmic exercises.

G. Surface

Aerobics should ideally be performed on a suspended wood floor, which provides a cushion of air between wood and concrete, or on high density mat-type aerobic flooring. If jogging on concrete is unavoidable, mats should be used or low impact movements should be utilized.

H. Heart Rate

Monitoring heart rate serves as a guideline to the level of exertion.

1. **Where** to take your pulse
   a. Carotid artery: Place index and middle finger by outside corner of eye and slide them straight down to the neck. Do not press hard or place thumb on opposite side of neck at the same time as the blood flow could be impeded and accurate heart rate measurements would not be possible.
   b. Radial artery: Place the fingers on the inner wrist, just below the wrist bone, straight down from the base of the thumb. This method is preferred to the carotid pulse due to the possible depressant effect on the heart rate during palpation. Do not use thumb to take pulse as the thumb has its own pulse.

2. **How** to determine your heart rate
   a. Count—Count your heart rate for 10 seconds
   b. Multiply—Multiply this number by 6, and you will know what your heart rate is for one minute at that particular time.

3. **Resting** heart rate
   a. Averages—Average for women is 78-84 beats per minute. Average for men is 72-78. A person in good aerobic condition generally has a lower resting heart rate.
   b. How to determine your resting heart rate—Take pulse for three mornings while still lying down, but after heart rate has settled down if awakened by an alarm. Add these three numbers together and then divide the answer by three. This number is your resting heart rate.

4. **Maximum** heart rate
   Theoretical maximum rate at which your heart can beat at your age. The mathematical constant 220 minus your age equals your ESTIMATED maximum heart rate. Do not exercise at this rate!
5. **Target** heart rate
   a. Purpose: Provides an easily indentifiable gauge of an individual's level of aerobic work and whether or not the intensity of aerobic activities should be increased or decreased.
   b. To determine target heart rate: Subtract your age from 220 and multiply this number by .6 and .85. This is your target heart rate range or zone that you shall "target" during aerobic exercise. Individuals with special needs (i.e., pregnant women or anyone with a history of any cardiopulmonary problem) should consult a physcian regarding the recommended target heart rate. When beginning an aerobics program, it is recommended that all individuals train at the lower end of their range for the first eight to ten weeks.
6. **Application**
   The pulse should be quickly located after vigorous exercise. Keep walking and take a 10-second count. Multiplying by six, this number should be in your individualized target zone. If it is higher or lower than the acceptable limits of your range, you will need to adjust the intensity of your exercise accordingly by being more or less vigorous.
7. **Monitoring** heart rate during aerobics
   In the most ideal of situations, AFAA recommends the taking of heart rate five minutes after the beginning of active aerobic work to determine if participant is working within his/her target zone. However, as taking heart rate at this time is not always feasible, heart rate should be checked at the completion of aerobic work rather than not at all.
8. **Recovery** heart rate
   a. Purpose: A recovery heart rate can indicate an individual's fitness level by the speed at which it returns to a pre-exercise level. It is also an indicator of whether the cool-down period was sufficient, and whether exercise intensity was appropriate. After five minutes, the heart rate should equal less than 60 percent of the maximum (220 minus age, multiplied by .6).

VIII. Post-Aerobic Cooldown

A. Purpose

To provide a transition period between vigorous aerobic work and musclar strengthening exercises or stretches. Without a gradual cool-down period, the blood which is pooled in the extremities immediately after an aerobic workout does not return to the heart as quickly or efficiently. Moderate to slow, rhythmic limbering movements for the upper and lower body will enable the muscles of the extremities to pump the blood back to the heart and brain. Stopping motionless after an aerobic workout could result in fainting.

B. Time

2-3 minutes of decreasing aerobic work such as walking, marching or other rhythmic activities.

C. Breathing

Breathing should be relaxed with rate and depth dictated by physiological reflexes. Students should learn to be aware of their own oxygen requirements and learn to regulate their breathing accordingly.

D. Stretches

After 2-3 minutes, the calves, front of lower leg and hamstrings should be statically stretched before proceeding with other exercises or rest.

E. Heart Rate

As an added precaution, AFAA recommends that the heart rate be again checked before beginning floor work. Heart rate should not exceed 60 percent of maximum (220 minus age multiplied by .6), five minutes after aerobic work. If heart rate is too high, continue walking slowly until heart rate has lowered sufficiently.

IX. Standing Abdominal Exercise

A. Purpose
To strengthen the abdominal muscles in a standing position.
1. Primary Muscles and Joint Action
   Rectus abdominis: anterior spinal flexion
   External and internal obliques: anterior spinal flexion,
   lateral flexion and rotation

B. Time
5 minutes

C. Method
Exercises should be performed in a controlled manner at a
moderate speed with an effort made to create resistance for
the working muscles. The lower torso remains motionless in
order to isolate upper body movement. Exercises such as
overhead reaches, quick side-to-side bends or fast waist
punches are ineffective for strengthening the abdominals.

D. Body Alignment
In order to protect the back from possible injury, care should
be taken to correctly align the body as described in Section I, C.
1. Lateral Flexion
   Stand with feet shoulder width apart, knees bent and
   buttocks tucked. Head should remain in midline position
   with shoulders and hips facing forward and squared.
   When working to the side, shoulder should drop directly
   to side, not to the front or back. Rib cage should remain
   open and uplifted to avoid collapsing in an unsupported
   movement to one side as this can cause unnecessary strain
   on the lower back. Lower torso should remain motionless
   with hips square to isolate the upper body and avoid
   stress to the knees.
2. Twisting
   If twisting the upper torso, knees should remain bent and
   always aligned over the feet, not turned in. Weight
   should be over the balls of the feet. Twisting exercises
   should be performed smoothly, not forcefully, with the
   lower torso motionless to prevent knee torque while
   twisting upper body.

E. Exercises to avoid
   The following exercises can create stress to the ligaments of
   the lower back and should be considered inappropriate for
   most individuals:
   1. Lateral flexion with both arms raised overhead.
   2. Any ballistic movement where the upper torso is
      unsupported.
   3. Windmill exercises in a forward flexed position either
      elbow to knee or traditional hand to toe.
   4. Upper body swings from one side to the other in a flat
      back, forward flexed position.

X. Legs, Hips and Buttocks Exercise

A. Purpose
   To strengthen the muscles of the legs, hips and buttocks.

B. Time
   10-15 minutes

C. Hips and Outer Thigh, Side Lying Position
   1. Primary Muscles and Joint Action
      Tensor fascia latae, gluteus medius: hip abduction
   2. Alignment and Method
      Body should be in a straight line, with supporting arm
      positioned squarely on the floor under shoulder; rib cage
      lifted so that the torso does not collapse. Shoulders and
      hips should remain square during the execution of any of
      the exercises with hips neither leaning to the front nor
      rolled backward onto buttocks. Use top arm to help sup-
      port the upper body. Lower leg should be relaxed and
      both legs aligned so knees are "stacked" for any of the
      outer thigh variations. When extending the leg, extend
      directly to the side, without locking the knee. To isolate
      the outer thigh and hip, resistance should be concen-
      trated on the lift and not the downward motion. Do not
      lift leg any higher than possible without altering align-
      ment. Use the "L" position with caution as this strains
      the gluteus medius tendon origin.

3. Common Problems
   - rolling back on hip
   - supporting elbow too close or too far out from shoulder
   - low back arched
   - "slouching" over supporting arm, causing rib cage to contract, rather than be lifted
   - lifting top leg too high to throw the body out of alignment
   - using momentum rather than controlled resistance
   - rolling hips too far forward
   - twisting upper torso so shoulders are not square

D. Hips and Outer Thigh—"hydrant position"
1. Primary muscles and Joint Action
   Tensor fascia latae, gluteus medius: hip abduction
2. Alignment and Method
   On all fours, head should be held in a natural extension of the spine, not hanging down. Hands should face forward and elbows should be slightly released, not locked. Hips remain square and weight should be balanced evenly between supporting leg and leg to be lifted without leaning to the side to compensate for lack of strength or to achieve greater height.
   Abdominals must be held in firmly with the pelvis tilted so that the lower back doesn't sway inward. Lift leg directly to the side. Knee remains pointing forward. Lift the leg only as high as is possible with the hips square and without leaning over onto the supporting leg. Avoid straight leg lifts directly to the side as this position puts a lot of pressure on the low back and is difficult to do and still maintain proper alignment. All outer thigh work performed in this position should be slow and controlled without using momentum to gain height.
3. Common Problems
   - leaning to one side
   - using momentum to lift leg
   - lifting leg too high and not directly to side

- dropping head down
- using torso movement rather than isolating the leg that is being lifted.
- sway back
- locking elbows

E. Inner Thigh—Side Lying Position

1. Primary Muscles and Joint Action
Adductors longus, brevis and magnus, gracilis, pectineus: hip adduction.

2. Alignment
Body should be in a straight line, shoulders and hips are square. The most effective position is to lie all the way down with head resting on forearm, top leg relaxed on floor. This allows the inner thigh to be isolated with the bottom leg extended directly to the side. Movement of inner leg is upward in a resistive manner. If using a position where the torso is raised and supported by forearm, bring top leg over working leg, keep foot flat on floor and lower leg in a straight vertical line.

3. Common Problems
   - rolling hips back so weight is on buttocks
   - holding bottom leg either too far forward or too far behind torso; should be extended directly to side
   - turning toe of bottom leg up so that the quadriceps are used or turning toe downward so that the hamstrings are used
   - using the torso and not isolating the leg lift, using momentum

F. Inner Thigh—Back Lying Position

1. Primary Muscles and Joint Action
adductors longus, brevis, and magnus, gracilis, pectineus: hip adduction

2. Alignment
Lie on back with legs vertically raised in air, shoulder width apart. Knees can be bent in toward chest or only slightly relaxed.
If legs are too far apart, it requires the use of the hip flexors to bring the legs close enough together to isolate the inner thigh muscles, which may cause the back to arch off floor.

3. Movement
Bring knees together, resisting motion in toward body's midline with hands on inside of thighs, relaxed at sides. It is important to control speed so that exercises remain resistive without the use of momentum.
4. Common Problems
   - arching back off floor
   - using ballistic moves downward, rather than resisting in toward midline of body
   - legs dropped too far forward, causing strain on lower back
   - legs should be directly vertical either with bent or straight knee

G. Buttocks—On Knees Position
1. Primary Muscles and Joint Action
gluteus maximus and minimus: hip extension
2. Alignment
On all fours, when working one leg to the back, the hips should be square and the back straight, not swayed. Abdominals should be contracted. Head is in alignment with spine, elbows are slightly bent, not hyperextended.
3. Movement
Leg lifts should be small and resistive with no torso movement involved. Avoid jerking or throwing the leg up as this can stress the lower back. Balance weight between supporting leg and leg that is extended. If leg extends higher than hips, drop to elbows. In either position, emphasis is on the "up" movement against gravity, tightening the gluteals with each lift. Avoid exercises which will arch and hyperextend the back, or use momentum, such as the donkey kick.
4. Common Problems
   - arching back
   - raising leg higher than hip in either position
   - torso movement, any momentum
   - head dropped, abdominals not lifted

H. Buttocks — Supine Position
1. Primary Muscles and Joint Action
gluteus maximus and minimus: hip flexion and extension

2. Alignment
When lying on back, knees should be bent and feet flat
on floor at a comfortable distance from body. Back
should not arch or sway in. Pelvis should be tilted and
abdominals tight so that the midline remains in contact
with the floor throughout entire movement.

3. Movement
The gluteal muscles should be contracted and released
without jerking or bouncing the pelvis up and down.
This is an excellent exercise, when performed with
abdominal curls to strengthen the pelvic girdle and
its attachments.

4. Common Problems
• using back rather than pelvis for lift
• arching lower back off floor
• arching rib cage
• lower body not aligned with knees over toes

I. Quadricep Strengthening Exercise

1. Primary Muscles and Joint Action
Quadricep femoris group: vastus lateralis, medialis, and
intermedius, rectus femoris, sartorius:
hip flexion, knee extension

2. Alignment and Movement
The quadriceps can be strengthened either in the standing position (squats and lunges), or in a sitting or supine
position (leg lifts and knee extensions).

a. Standing Position
In a standing position, use basic guidelines for body
alignment. Knees should be relaxed and aligned over
toes, buttocks tucked, abdominals contracted, and rib
cage lifted. Do not collapse upper torso. Shoulders
should remain up and back in a relaxed position.
When bending, hips should always be higher than
knees. Overbending, or bending too low may cause
stress to the ligaments of the knee.

b. Sitting or Supine Position
Quadricep strengthening can be accomplished by
either sitting in a chair or on the floor, or lying on the
back. The upper torso should be maintained in a supported position, shoulders up and back. Use slow, controlled, resistive movement to perform knee extensions

or straight leg lifts. Avoid jerking or throwing of leg.
Note that rotation of the leg within the hip joint will
emphasize work of different muscles within the
quadriceps group.
3. Common Problems
  • using momentum rather than a controlled lift
  • hyperextension of knee joint when performing
    extensions
  • arching the back
  • using hip flexors to lift leg
  • dropping hips below the knees during a squat

J. Hamstring Strengthening Exercise

1. Primary Muscles and Joint Action
   Hamstring group: biceps femoris, semitendinosus,
   semimembranosis;
   knee flexion, hip flexion

2. Alignment
   Hamstring strengthening occurs when performing straight leg lifts
   or bent knee curls behind the body.
   When strengthening a hamstring in a standing position,
   follow guidelines outlined for quadriceps in a standing
   position. Hamstrings will also be strengthened as the opposing muscle group, when performing squats.
   To strengthen hamstrings on all fours, follow guidelines
   outlined for buttocks. Strengthening will occur with a
   controlled straight leg lift to the rear or on all fours, curl-
   ing heel of foot toward buttocks in a resistive manner.

3. Common Problems
   • arching back
   • using quadriceps or hip flexor to lift leg to the rear
     without tightening buttocks
   • raising hip in air
   • no resistance with a curl

XI. Supine Abdominal Exercise

A. Purpose
To strengthen the abdominal muscles and provide support for
the internal organs and the back.

1. Primary Muscles and Joint Action
   Rectus abdominis: spinal flexion
   External and internal obliques: lateral spinal flexion, rotation

B. Time

5-8 minutes

C. Alignment

In order to isolate the abdominal muscles, an abdominal curl which flexes the spine approximately 25-45 degrees will contract these muscles sufficiently to improve strength and tone. Lie on the floor, supine, with knees bent, feet flat on floor and pelvis tilted so that the low back and rib cage are flat and pressed to floor. A curl will bring the head, shoulders and rib cage up and forward in a slow and controlled motion without momentum. Do not lift with just the neck and push the head out of alignment. Head should be fully supported without any neck movement. Return to starting position without dropping head and shoulders on floor. Maintain a constant contraction in the abdominals throughout exercise. Strengthen the external and internal obliques by including exercises that involve a twist with the lower torso stable and motionless.

D. Arm Positions

When supporting the head, do not clasp and interlock fingers behind neck. This position does not offer support if you are pressing forward on neck or the head hangs down behind neck in a hyperextended position. Place spread fingers on the back of the head for the best support. Arms may also be extended up and/or out in front of body as long as the head and neck are aligned as an extension of the spine. Other variations include crossing arms in front of chest, or fingers on forehead with elbows forward.

E. Abdominal Work vs. Hip Flexor Work

During a full sit-up, the first 40 degrees of the movement relies on the abdominals. However, the remainder of the movement towards a full sitting position depends on the hip flexors (iliopsoas muscles). When lying on the back and performing any exercises that lift one or both legs, the hip flexor will be involved in the work. Never lift both legs off the floor at the same time as this can place tremendous strain on the low back, even if the hands are underneath the buttocks.

F. Breathing

Breathing is especially important while performing abdominal exercises. Exhale while contracting the abdominals at the point of finishing your greatest exertion. **Example: Exhale at the top of the sit-up, inhale when you lie back down.**

G. **Variety**

Vary your abdominal exercises. Six minutes of bent knee sit-ups is not only boring but insufficient to work the entire abdominal area. Exercises that include changing the position of the leg, i.e., bent into the chest, lifted vertical in the air, elbow to knee twists, or reverse sit-ups will work the abdominal muscles effectively and isolate these muscle groups without the use of momentum.

H. Common Problems
- arching the low back off the floor
- arching the rib cage
- using neck motion only
- unsupported head
- jerky movements
- not bringing shoulders and upper torso off the floor
- when breathing, pushing the abdominal muscles out

XII. Cool-Down Stretches

A. **Purpose**

To increase muscle flexibility and relieve any metabolic waste accumulated in muscles from strengthening activities.

B. **Time**

4-6 minutes at the very end of class.

C. **Stretching**

Follow the same basic guidelines as outlined for stretches at the beginning of your class. Static stretch is the most effective at the end of your class when your muscles are very warm and prepared to stretch a little farther than at the beginning of your class. Now is the time to work on increasing flexibility, holding stretches a little longer, stretching a little farther to relax the muscle.

D. **Muscle Groups**

Stretch all major muscle groups that were used during the workout especially the calves, hamstrings, and quadriceps. Stretches for the back should also be included. Include exercises that will balance muscle groups, improve posture and body alignment.

E. Breathing

Inhale as you begin the stretch, and simultaneously stretch and relax the muscle as you exhale.

XIII. Final Heart Rate

A. Purpose

To determine if heart rate has sufficiently returned to normal pre-exercise ranges.

B. When

Should be taken as stretches are finished and class members prepare to leave.

C. Heart Rate

Again, the recovery heart rate equals 60 percent of maximum (220 minus age, multiplied by .6). If not below this level, the individual was probably exercising too intensely and should work at a less vigorous level during the next class. Cooldown stretches should be continued until heart rate is lowered.

D. Saunas and Hot Tubs

Saunas, hot tubs and even hot showers, should be avoided immediately following exercise. The heat causes the blood vessels to dilate and this, along with the fact that the blood tends to be pooled in the extremities following vigorous exercise, causes the heart and brain to receive less blood.

E. Hydration and Rehydration

Overheating can be a serious problem and special precautions should be taken, particularly in hot weather. Individuals who exercise need to replenish their water to maintain electrolyte balance. For every twenty minutes of exercise, allow 3 ounces of water. Salt tablets are not necessary unless involved in heavy endurance events and should not be taken without consultation with a sport physician or nutritionist. Deliberate dehydration by wearing heavy, rubberized clothes to induce profuse sweating is not recommended. This weight loss is temporary and will be regained through appropriate hydration.